VATICAN ART

VATICAN ART

BY

KARL IPSER

WITH 160 ILLUSTRATIONS

Translated from the German "Die Kunstwerke des Vatikans"
by DOIREANN MacDERMOTT
B. A. University of London

PHILOSOPHICAL LIBRARY
NEW YORK

Published, 1953, by Philosophical Library, Inc.

15 East 40th Street, New York 16, N. Y.

Printed in Spain for the Philosophical Library Inc.

by Imprenta Moderna, Barcelona

THE VATICAN

There is no place in the world equal to the Vatican in historical and cultural importance. Within a very small area, which nowhere measures more than 1100 yards across, lies the seat of a world-wide empire. This unique power has survived wars, revolutions, disasters, schisms, the dominations of hostile, foreign princes and the eventual decline of its own spiritual, fighting force. From all these various things it seems to have acquired a new inner strength. It is a power which has had a remarkable and important influence over mankind and all the things of this world for nearly two thousand years, uniting, as it does, some four hundred million souls. It dates back to the time of Peter, the fisherman, who was crucified under this very cupola, and his 261 successors represent, to catholics, the authority which has been imposed between man and God as a medium between this world and the next. The Vatican is, therefore, not only a state with two thousand citizens, but it is also the home of Christ's tenets, a place of adoration and veneration, the centre of a world-wide religion and, consequently, of a world-wide power. This accounts for the singular feeling we get on looking once again at St. Peter's within whose mighty shadow lies the Vatican, that palace which the greatest artists of Christendom have embellished with their most important work. It is from here that the greatest moral force works along with the times. On an area of a quarter of a square kilometer, the eternal city of Rome has survived throughout the ages. It is from here that the Popes survey the mighty expanse of the Eternal City.

Thick, unsurmountable walls separate the Vatican City from Rome, and enclose the many buildings with their courtyards, staircases, their thousand rooms and chapels and the famous Vatican Garden where the Pope finds relaxation from his responsible work. It was in the quiet, spacious rooms of the Papal Palace that the great masters of the 15th., 16th., and 17th. centuries realised their artistic ideas and dreams.

In the year 498, Pope Symmachus, started building a palace on Mount Vatican, the «Hill of Predications», in order that he might have a residence in the vestibulo of the old Basilica. Emperors and princes have stayed here before their coronations, among others, Charles and Otto the Great. In 1150 Pope Eugene III erected a new building, but the Lateran remained the Papal residence. It was only when they returned from their French exile and found the Lateran in ruins, that the Popes established the Vatican as their official dwelling. In the course of time the palace was extended into a whole network of buildings. The extensive plans of Pope Nicholas V, who about the year 1450 proposed building an entire papal city, were only partially realised by his successors and the architects Bramante, Fontana, Bernini and Simonetti. The palace is, in the main, a Renaissance creation and its interior also has been furnished in that spirit by its great masters.

Anyone, therefore, wishing to learn something of the spirit, art and culture of the Renaissance, should, above all, direct his attention to the Vatican.

The private apartments and reception rooms of the Pope and his retinue occupy but a small part of the whole. The rest, the museums of sculpture, the Stanzes, the Loggias, the Borgia Apartment, the Pinacothek, the Lateran, the archives and the unique library, has all been most generously opened to the public.

The richness of the art collections is unbounded. Hellas and ancient Rome arise here with a vital force which exceeds all imagination. Beginning with the most ancient works, the four thousand year old Egyptian stone images, all the skill and genius of nations far and wide have found a home within this marvellous centre. Gods and heroes of ancient Greece, strange works of the Etruscans and Romans, early christian and mediaeval art all seem to blossom anew. The pure, delicate paintings of Fra Angelico, Perugino and Boticelli are followed by monuments of the majestic Bramante, Michaelangelo, Raffael and the successors of Bernini to Canova. It is an immeasurable collection of marvellous creations which an individual can only digest gradually, one by one. The Vatican has always been a centre and collecting-place of the best artistic elements of all times and, consequently, it has become familiar even to those people who would otherwise have no connection with it whatever.

The painstaking efforts of the Church which has, for 400 years, been untiringly and lovingly gathering together works of art, are very much to be admired. She has spared no means or effort to assemble, restore and maintain them for the furtherance of the enlightenment, instruction, pleasure, elevation and knowledge of mankind. Truly inspired by divine grace, the Popes have thrown open their homes and palaces to all men, giving art every opportunity of developing Laymen, artists, men of letter may find here the history and evolution of people of all times. The Vatican has, therefore, become of the highest value in the spiritual development of the whole world.

ST. PETER'S

The history of St. Peter's is really the history of Christendom. On the place where, only a few years after the crucifixion of St. Peter, bishop Anacletus had erected an oratory, Constantine the Great, according to ancient tradition, built the first Basilica at about the beginning of the 4th. century. When this was destroyed, the Popes decided on a new building which was started under Pope Nicholas V in 1452 and was continued under Pope Paul II. St. Peter's is the most tremendous task ever put before an architect and generations of artists, from Bramante to Bernini, have by their skill wrought all the mighty power of the Popes into a harmonious whole.

Pope Julian II directed Bramante who, in 1506, began the work. After the outer courtyards of the old Basilica — except for the Choir-apse with St. Peter's Altar — had been pulled down, the foundation stone of the new edifice was laid (with great pomp) on the 18th. of April, 1506, near the actual cupola column with St. Veronica's statue. Bramante's plan was to have an equilateral Greek cross with an immense cupola in the centre and four smaller ones in the corners. Unfortunately this original plan has been altered — a plan which has never been equalled by any edifice of ancient times in the majesty and greatness of its spirit. It was, like all perfect things, simple and sincere. In spite of the huge dimensions nothing had been left to chance; the principles were carefully formulated. In the harmonious unity of his mighty curves the force of gravity seems to be defied and no one can deny the magic of this material transformed into such beateous form.

After the death of Bramante, the 31 year old Raffael took over the direction. He designed the longhouse demanded by the opponents of the scheme, and hollowed out the arcades leading to the small cupolas the southern cross. After his death, A. di Sangallo, who died in 1546, continued the work, first as a round edifice, but he afterwards decided upon a long nave. In 1546 the work was given to the 72 year old Michaelangelo. His plan reverted to that of Bramante with some modifications. He needed all his fame and had to renounce his fee before he could enforce his plan. When he died the building was nearly complete apart from the facade. For the cupola he designed a wooden model which can still be seen today and which was never opposed by succeeding generations. It was completed in 1950 by Giacomo della Porta with the help of Domenico Fontana. With it was realised the most ambitious architectural conception, a worthy coronation of the lifework of Michaelangelo and the Renaissance. As a follower of Bramante he succeeded in filling hitherto unknown proportions with beauty and imagination. The arms of the cross bear up the cupola like two gigantic arches rising up in triumph. The dimensions between its columns and arcades, the contrast between its straight foundations and the enormous arches produces a vital rhythm and pliant span of curve which is not found in any other cupola. This cupola is the huge and impressive head of the cathedral. It is the symbol and glory of Rome, visible from the Pincio and the bridges and from all the bends of the river Tiber and all the hills of the Eternal City. It is the guiding star, the centre and symbol of a venerated dream of mankind which has become a reality.

In 1606, forty years after the completion of the central structure, Pope Paul V commissioned C. Maderna to add a nave. He wanted to make a larger space for big ceremonies and to cover the whole area of the sacred ground of the old Basilica with this new building. Maderna reduced the total width of the structure to a minimum and consequently the side naves became too small and had to be sub-divided into oval, domed rooms which are continued by the chapels in the form of flat niches. He also designed a new façade which became a monumental piece of decoration being completely detached from the cupola and main-building. Viewed from the front the cupola is reduced to half its size and inside, the central and posterior arms can only be seen after one has traversed half the nave. It was Maderna, also, who created the famous vestibulum with its well-known stucco ceiling covered with reliefs. On the clearly illuminated ends are, right, the equestrian statue of Charles the Great and, left, that of Constantine the Great. Over the central doorway is the famous «Navicella» (the little ship), a mosaic by Giotto, transferred here from the old Basilica. The Church is sailing like a ship in a storm while Peter walks over the waves to Christ. From the vestibulum there are five doorways opening on to the church. The Porta Argenta is only opened on special holidays. It still bears the old bronze wings of the ancient Basilica which were made at the time of Pope Eugene IV (1439-1447). The last door on the right is the Porta Santa.

After Maderna's death in 1629, the young Bernini was entrusted with the task of carrying on the work. However, his immeasurable and superficial work did not continue the masterpiece begun by Bramante and Michaelangelo. It was only forty years later, as an old man, that he created the colonnades, thus perfecting the work of centuries with his spacious art. It so happened by some trick of perspective he managed to weaken the already unfortunate impression of the façade. By putting the two ends of the hall, from which the broad façade rises, close together, he has produced an optical illusion about the elevation of the square and one has the impression that one is on the same level as the colonnades. If the ends of the hall were wider apart than the façade this illusion would not exist. The elliptical position of the colonnades has also produced an illusion that the square is larger than it really is.

«St. Peter's has certainly been planned on as mighty a scale as one of the old temples, indeed much mightier and more audacious, and here before us lies not only what two thousand years has destroyed but also what a better enlightenment could again produce.»

PINACOTECA VATICANA

The Pinacoteca, founded by Pope Pius VII, originally contained only 42 masterpieces. With time this collection has been enlarged by pictures from the Library, from the Gallery of the Lateran and from various rooms of the Vatican. It is considered as one of the richest in Rome.

1st. Room.

2. St. Francis of Assisi by Margaritone d'Arezzo (1216-1293). The picture was painted in the lifetime of the saint who was personally know to the artist.
526. The Last Judgement by Giovanni and Niccolo, Benedictine monks of the 11th. century. These are the oldest paintings in Italy.

2nd. Room.

165. Christ blessing by Simone di Martini di Siena (1285-1344).
196 to 201. The works of Charity. by Lorenzo Monaco (1370-1425).

3rd. Room.

243. Coronation of St. Mary by Filippo Lippi. Dates 1460.
247-250. Scenes from the life of St. Nicholas of Bari by Gentile da Fabriano.
251-252. Scenes from the life of St. Nicholas of Bari, birth, preaching and miracles by Fra Angelico (1378-1455).
262. St. Thomas receiving the girdle from the Virgin. by Benozzo Gozzoli (1420-1497).

5th. Room.

275. The lamentation of Christ by Lucas Cranach (1472-1553).
286. The Miracles of St. Vicent Ferrar, by Fr. Cossa of Ferrara (1435-1477).
279. The Virgin, a present of the Auditorium of Ruota, by Ant. Romano (1460-1508.

6th. Room.

297. Virgin with Child, by Carlo Crivelli, worked 1468-1493.
298. Virgin with Child and Saints, by the same.
299. Altarpiece with the Crucifixion, by Niccolo Alunno. da Forligno (1430-1502).
307. Altar from Montelpare, by Crivelli or Alunno, dat. 1466.
303. St. Antony between priests and saints, by Ant. Vivarini, dat. 1469.

7th. Room.

312. Coronation of the Virgin, by Pinturrichio (1434-1513).
317. Virgin between Saints, by Perugino (1446-1524). He was the teacher of Raffael d'Urbino.
318. Resurrection, by the same.

10th. Room.

346. Allegory by Paolo Veronese (1528-1588).
350. St. Bernardus by Sebastiano del Piombo (1485-1547). He was a pupil of Michaelangelo.
351. Madonna di San Niccolo di Frari. The Saints Sebastian, Francis, Peter, Ambrose and Catherine before a shrine upon which the Virgin appears with the Child. By Titian (1477-1576).
354. St. George by Paris Bordone (1500-1571).
359. Madonna da Monteluce and Coronoation of the Virgin by Cuilio Romano and Franc. Penni (1492-1546) and (1488-1522).

11th. Room.

368. The Resurrection of Lazarus by Girolamo Muziano da Brescia (1528-1590).
376. The Annunciation to the Virgin by Fed. Barocci (1526-1612).

12th. Room.

381. Martyrdom of SS. Processus and Martinianus by Valentin (1501-1634). After a mosaic in St. Peter's.
383. The Incredulous Thomas by Guercino da Cento (1591-1666).
384. The communion of St. Jerome by Domicchino (1581-1641).
387. Crucifixion of St. Peter by Guido Reni (1575-1642).
388. Holy Family by G. M. Crespi, «Lo Spagnuolo» (1665-1747).
389. The Virgin between two saints by Guido Reni.
391. St. Mary Magdalene by Guercino.
394. Martyrdom of St. Erasmus by Nic. Poussin (1594-1665). See mosaic at St. Peter's.

13th. Room.

397. Madonna with Child by Carlo Maratta d'Ancona (1625-1713).
405. The Virgin appearing to St. Francis by Pietro da Cortona (1596-1669).
775. St. Francis Xavier by van Dyck (1599-1641).
1059. Judith by Gentileschi da Pisa (1562-1647).

14th. Room.

416, 418, 441, 443. Legends and flowers by Daniel Seghers (1590-1661). He
   was a pupil of Jan Brueghel jr.
432 to 439. Astronomy by Donati Creti (1671-1749).

15th. Room.

448. George IV of England by Thomas Lawrence (1769-1830). A masterpiece
   of that famous English portrait-painter.
458. Pope Benedict XIV by M. C. Crespi. This picture shows the cardinal
   and was changed after his election as Pope.
460. Pope Clement IX by Carlo Maratta. A picture copied many times.
1210. Pope Gregory XII by Muziano. An idealised portrait (1528-1590).

SALA A CROCE GRECA (The Hall in the form of a Greek Cross)

This was constructed by the architect M. A. Simonetti under Pope Pius VI
(1775-1799), in the form of a Greek Cross. On the floor are three ancient mosaics from the 2nd. and 3rd. centuries. A. D. A shield with Minerva's head
a marvellous flower basket and a Bacchus. Over the architrave is a relief with
two gladiators fighting against lions and tigers. The doorway is red oriental
granite. By the entrance 578 and 579: Two Sphinxes of granite similar but
of different origin. Ist. 2nd. Cent. A. D.
567. A woman's figure in the style of the 5th. cent. B. C. with a strange head
   perhaps Cleopatra (74-30 B.C.).
566. Sarcophagus in alabaster of Costanza, daughter of Constantine the Great.
   Relief decoration with flowers, grapes and the genius of grapepicking.
   4th. cent. A. D. The vine is a symbol of Christ, the peacock that of
   immortality and the ram that of the Good Shepherd.
589. Sarcophagus in porphyry from the mausoleum of St. Helena, mother of
   Constantine the Great. Pope Anastasius IV intended it for his tomb
   in the Lateran. Pope Pius VI put it in the Vatican. The relief pre-
   sents knights, dispersed prisoners, barbarians and death. On the sides
   portraits of St. Helena and Constantine. 4th. cent. A. D.
597. Gaius Caesar, nephew of Augustus, as Pontifex Maximus. 20 B. C.
   to 4 A. D.
564. Lucius Verus the younger. 161-169 A. D.
565. Augustus. Body in the style of the 5th. cent. B. C.

THE SALA ROTUNDA

541. Faustina, the younger, wife of Antonius Pius. Died 141 A. D.
542. Colosal statue of a goddess, perhaps Demeter as a great and venerable
   matron. Replica of a Greek original from 5th. B. D.

543. Bust of Hadrian from his mausoleum. 117-138 A. D.
545. Giant bust of Antonius (See photo).
548. Emperor Nerva represented as the enthroned Zeus. There are few other portrait-busts in Roman art which can be compared with this one as far as truth and greatness of conception is concerned. Ist. cent. A. D.
550. Giant statue of Claudius as Jupiter. Governed 41-54 A. D.
551. Head of Claudius.
552. Juno Sospita. The goddess was venerated in Lanuvium and hence her name Juno Lanuvium. As protectress of herds she bears a shield and lance and her head and body are covered with furs. She has a temple at the Palatinus and the original of this replica in the greek-roman style from the 2nd. cent. A. D. was in a temple at Lanuvium. Restored after old coins.
553. Portrait of Plotina, wife of Trajan. Died 122 A. D.
554. Head of an empress, perhaps Julia Domna, 2nd. cent. A. D. The greatest conserved head of a woman of ancient times. She was a syrian the second wife of emperor Septimus Severus and mother of Caracalla.
555. Genius of Augustus with a veil on the back of his head and a horn of riches.
556. A so-called Pertinax. 3rd. Cent. A. D.

GALLERIA DELLE STATUE

At the entrance is the tombstone of a young man to whom a slave gives a bottle of oil and a scraper that he may cleanse himself of the dust of the wrestling arena. Marvellous Greek original of the 5th. cent. B. C.

255. The judgement of Paris. Replica after Greek original of 4th. cent. B. C.
270. Muse restored as Urania. From a group of Muses in the Sala delle Muse.
395. Apollo Kitharoedos. Replica of a archaic original of 5th. cent. B. C.
398. Opelius Macrinus (Gov. 217-218). The only remaining statue of this emperor who was the assassin and successor of Caracalla.
404. Tombstone of a certain Liberata Fania Nicopoli. Roman original of the 2nd. cent. A. D.
417. Hermes. Roman replica of a Greek original of 5 th. cent. B. C.
420. Lucius Verus. The head is one of the best portraits of this emperor. The body is a work of the Ist. Cent. A. D.

In the centre of the room a great bath of oriental alabaster found in Rome in 1853.

THE VATICAN. — The Mediaeval walls are clearly visible apart from St. Peter's Square. The white stripe along the ground indicates the frontier. The State of the Vatican City is the smallest state in the world with an area of only 44 ha. nearly a quarter of which is built over. The Vatican State is an elective monarchy governed authoritatively but without a constitution. Like any other state it has its own passports and ambassadors car number-plates, post, radio, a railway with 950 yards of track, a bank, fire-brigade and prison. Diplomats appointed to the state live in Rome.

ST. PETER'S. — Everyone is welcome here. The colonnades open with an impelling power as if they would embrace the whole world. During the day, the marble halls offer ideal resting places for the onlooker and at night, they are discreetly lit by handwrought iron lamps, forming a magnificent surrounding for the square. This vestibilum to the most gigantic of God's houses is really a place of delight for all mankind. Standing midway between the every day world and the kingdom of faith, it at once calls the spectator to contemplation, preparing him for his entrance into the church and brings him back to the world again when he leaves it. View of the 19th. Cent.

VIEW OF ROME FROM ST. PETER'S. — The Vatican Borgo Nuovo was destroyed and today a forty yard wide street leads from the Tiber to the Vatican, the «Street of Peace» so-called in remembrance of the peace concluded between the Church and the Italian state by the signing of the Lateran Pact in 1929. The much discussed question of the street leading into the square was solved by building two, new, twin palaces on either side of it, thus reducing it to half its width. It is only after these propylaea that the square opens up to its full amplitude.

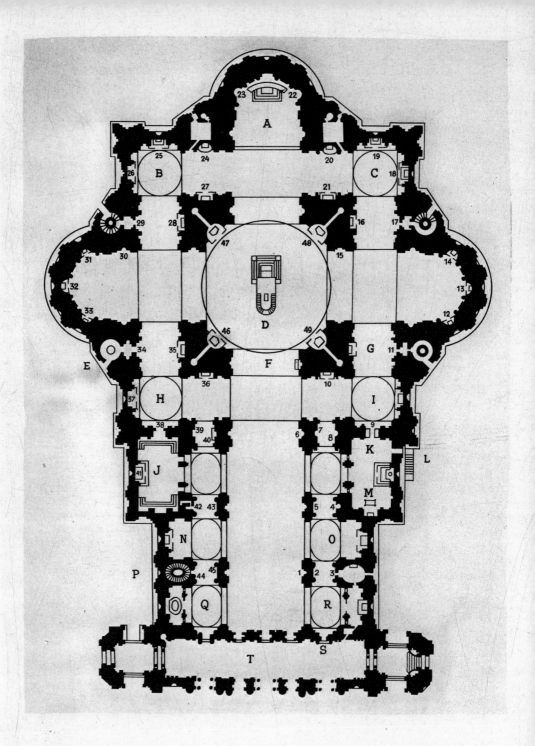

PLAN OF ST. PETER'S. — Bramante and Michaelangelo planned a central structure in the form of an equilateral cross with the cupola giving an impression of unity and compactness. The four arms of the cross are perfectly balanced and the light streams in in all directions from the cupola. Raffael Sangallo and other builders chose the long edifice such as we see today. The entrance is endowed by some strangely magic power with its striking contrast to the light which streams down from the cupola and which grows in intensity as we approach the centre.

EXPLANATION
OF GROUND-PLAN
OF THE
BASILICA OF SAN PETER

1. St. Theresa of Avila.
2. St. Christine of Sweden.
3. Pope Leo XII
4. Pope Innocent XII.
5. St. Mathilda of Tuscany.
6. St. Philip Neri.
7. Tomb of Pope Gregory XIV.
8. Tomb of Pope Gregory XIII.
9. Tomb of Pope Gregory XVI.
10. Mosaic of St. Jerome.
11. Tomb of Pope Benedict XIV.
12. Mosaic of St. Wenceslaus.
13. Mosaic of Sts Processus and Martinianus.
14. Mosaic of the martyrdom of St. Erasmus.
15. St. Bruno.
16. Altar of the «Navicella».
17. Pope Clement XIII.
18. Mosaic of the Archangel Michael.
19. Mosaic of St. Petronella.
20. Pope Clement X.
21. St. Peter resurrecting Tabitha.
22. Tomb of Pope Urban VIII.
23. Tomb of Pope Paul III.
24. Tomb of Pope Alexander VIII.

25. Altar of St. Leo.
26. Madonna della Colonna.
27. St. Peter curing the possessed.
28. The fall of Simon Magus.
29. Tomb. of Pope Alexander VII.
30. St. Norbert.
31. Altar and Mosaic of St. Thomas.
32. Mosaic of the crucifixion of St. Peter.
33. Mosaic of St. Valery.
34. Tomb of Pope Pius VIII.
35. Mosaic of the death of Ananias.
36. Mosaic of the Transfiguration.
37. Tomb of Pope Gregory de Great
38. Tomb of Pope Pius VII.
39. Tomb of Pope Leo XI.
40. Tomb of Pope Innocent XI.
41. Mosaic of the Annunciation.
42. Tomb of Pope Pius X
43. Tomb of Pope Innocent VIII.
44. Tomb of M. C. Sobiesky.
45. Tomb of the Stuarts
46. St. Andrew.
47. St. Veronica.
48. St. Helena.
49. St. Longinus.

A. St. Peter's Chair and Tribune.
B. Chapel of the Column.
C. Chapel of St Michael.
D. Main altar - Pius VI.
E. Entrance to the Sacristy.
F. Statue of St. Peter.
G. St. Basil
H. Clementine Chapel.
I. Gregorian Chapel.
J. Choir Chapel.

K. Chapel of the Holy Sacrament.
L. Entrance to the Popes Palace.
M. Tomb. of Pope Sixtus IV.
N. Chapel of the Presentation.
O. Chapel of St. Sebastian.
P. Staircase to the cupola.
Q. Baptistery.
R. Chapel of the Pietá.
S. Porta Santa.
T. Atrium.

EXPLANATION
OF GROUND-PLAN
OF THE
BASILICA OF SAN PETER

ATRIUM OF ST. PETER. — 225 ft. long, 40 ft. wide and 60 ft. high, it was constructed by C. Maderna. On the left is the statue of Charles the Great, and on the right that of Constantine the Great by Bernini. Five doors open into the church. Over the central doorway the «Navicella» of Giotto represents the church in the form of a ship being tossed by the storm. Peter walks quietly over the waves to meet his Lord. The bronze panels of the door are the work of Anonio Filarete, its reliefs representing scenes from the life of Christ and from mythology. The door with the cross is the Porta Santa. The roof is adorned with policromed reliefs by Maderna.

BRONZE STATURE OF ST. PETER. — This world famous statue is certainly of the early christian period, 5th. cent., after the style of antique statues clad in togas. St. Peter is blessing with his right hand, in his left he has the key. His hair is short and curly and his beard rounded. This is the original image on which all later representations of the saint were based. Most probably a Byzantine emperor dedicated this work as a Christmas gift to the Church, but it was precisely this work which suffered under the odium of later, iconoclastic emperors of Byzantium and it was only in the time of Pope Paul V that it was transferred here from the monastery of St. Martin next door.

THE TOMB OF POPE PIUS VII. — This Pope (1800-1823) made a pact with Napoleon and crowned him Emperor. For this he was to suffer greatly and he was exiled. His tomb is simple and dignified. All the papal pomp has been stripped away and there is no splendour or outward show. Here sits a man whose high office made him all the more humble. He seems to hear inner voices. His right hand is raised in gentle admonition and the left rests wearily in his lap. To right and left of him are the spirits of Time and History and below, the virtues of Knowledge and Power. Work by the Danish master, Thorwaldsen.

THE CUPOLA OF ST. PETER. — This is the symbol and pride of the Eternal
City. It can be seen from all the bridges and towers, heights and every bend of the
river Tiber. It was Michaelangelo who crowned the most majestic cathedral of Christendom with this cupola, 400 ft. high and over 125 ft. wide. The building was completed
in 1590 and with it was realised the noblest edifice of the Renaissance.

THE CUPOLA OF ST. PETER'S. — A daring masterpiece. Michaelangelo heightened the line of Bramante's cupola but otherwise kept to the original plans. He specially devoted his attention to the arching itself and in this he succeeded in intensifying the feeling of majestic stillness. The great windows of the round dome flood the church with great streams of light. The monumental, stucco decorations by Bramante are incomparable. Above the friese is an attic with corinthian columns in pairs between sixteen windows of alternately rounded and pointed tops. Over these are sixteen flat ribs covered with gold stucco representing stars and lions heads. Between the ribs there are sixteen mosaics. The border is composed of a double cornice with sixteen small quadrangular windows. Above these is the lantern with three fasciae which serve as a base for the sixteen columns between sixteen round windows. At the top of all is God the Father with cherubs. The inscription runs: S. Petri Gloriae Sixtus PP. V. A. M. D. X. C. Pontif. V.

BRONZE BALDACHIN. — Over the tomb of St. Peter on the High Altar, or «Altare Papale», where only the Holy Father himself says Mass on Christmas, Easter and St. Peter's day. This is a work of Bernini and was consecrated by Pope Urban VIII in 1633. To make it the artist employed materials from the bronze decorations of the Pantheon. Thus the Romans made the saying: «What was not broken up by the Barbarians, was broken off by the Barberini». Bernini's aim was to build an altar which should be the centre of attention in spite of the vast dimensions of the church. He accomplished his with these wooden columns which have been described by famous art critics as «out of place and period».

BRAMANTE. — Originally a painter, educated at Milan, he was from 1500 in Rome. He was the pioneering spirit of architecture from whom all the followers learnt. His name is forever linked with those of St. Peter's and the Vatican. Unfortunately his ingenious project for the Vatican was only partly carried out. Otherwise it would have been a perfect building in its simple strength and severe beauty. Under the patronage of Pope Julian II he constructed the marvellous Belvedere with its beautiful staircase and portal arch of triumph in the Giardino della Pigna. Raffael, to whom he taught architecture, is indebted to Bramante for bringing him to the notice of Pope Julian II who encouraged the young master to the most outstanding work. But all this is as nothing when compared with the greatest and most gigantic of Bramante's works — St. Peter's. His plans have been copied many thousands of times in the architecture of the catholic world. All the later, even Michaelangelo, masters learned from him without ever becoming his equal. In Bramante all the forces of Italian Renaissance architecture were developed in the most classical style to their greatest flowering. The portrait is by a contemporary master, Giovanni Santi, the father of Raffael. It is at the Pinacothec of the Vatican.

THE PIETA BY MICHAELANGELO. — What a serene sadness lies upon the figure of the Mother and how restrained this expression of noble mourning. The head of Christ is equal to the best masterpieces of antiquity in its depths and tenderness. The body of the Son rests lightly on his Mother's lap. Suffering and pain have left no marks. The limbs fall easily into position and the head lies relaxed. Michaelangelo began this work when he was 23 years old and finished it within a year. It is the only one of his works which bears his name — on the band across the Mother's breast. There is only one other work to equal this in Christian times and that is his Moses from the tomb of Pope Julian II.

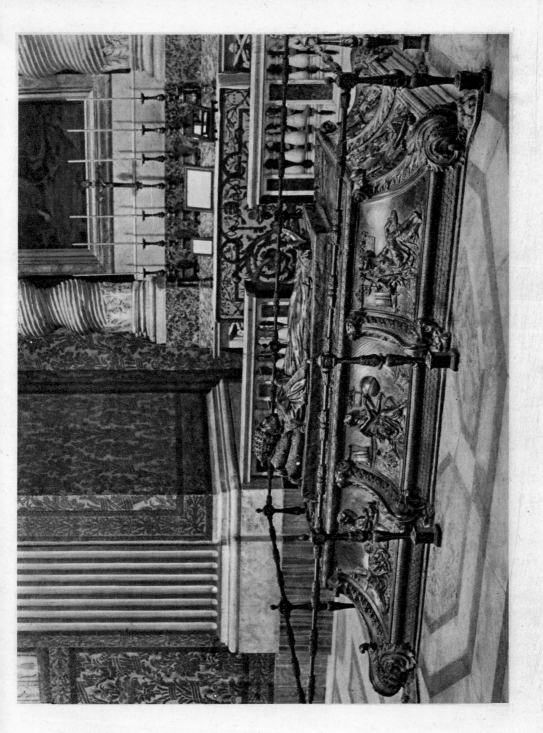

THE TOMB OF POPE SIXTUS IV. — A masterpiece of the early Roman Renaissance finished by Ant. Pollajualo in 1493. The constructor of the Capella Sixtina and co-founder of the Vatican Library has acquired a worthy monument. The bronze rises up as a black mass surmounted by the clear cut figure of the Pope. The base is ornamented with a relief showing the female figures of Arithmetic, Astrology, Dialectic, Rhetoric and Grammar, Perspective and Music, Geometry and Theology. In the corners are the papal coats-of arms. Next to him is buried Pope Julian II who erected this monument to his great uncle.

POPE SIXTUS IV AND PLATINA. — This is a mural transferred to canvas by Melozzo da Forli (1438-1494). The Pope is seated quietly with great dignity in his chair. Kneeling before him is the librarian Platina waiting to receive the bull, about the opening of the Vatican Library, from the Pope's hand. Beside the Pope are his nephews. On the right cardinal Giuliano della Rovere, later Pope Julian II and left, cardinal Pietro Riario. The masterly, characteristic portraits, the rich perspective architecture and the very beautiful, clear colours make this picture (completed in 1478) one of the greatest pictorial creations of the Italian Renaissance.

ANGEL MAKING MUSIC. — The enthusiastic movement and the liberty and intrepidity of expression which live in the heads of the angels and apostles of the wallpaintings is quite charming. The noble and innocent beauty of youth is here represented with a simplicity hitherto unknown in the 15th. cent. In these works of Melozzo da Forli the art of Upper Italy has once again reached its gracious intimacy combined with a masterly design, soft clarity of colour and a skillful use of perspective.

THE VIRGIN AND CHILD. — Fra Angelico (1378-1455) here gives expression to the intimate piety of the Middle Ages in the sublime purity of the faces and the noble figures. The Madonna is surrounded in the sweet atmosphere of an ideal life which also is reflected in the rosy, laughing features of the child. At the feet of the Virgin, St. Dominic and St. Catherine whose divinely inspired peace and quiet devotion seem to be of another world. The fresh and blooming colours, the marvellous fall of the robes and the delicate purity of execution illustrates the harmonious beauty of Fra Angelico's art which blossomed like a late flower in a new era. His masterly paintings are often, like miniatures, passed by unnoticed.

ST. JEROME. — The saint has fallen upon his knees in a very ecstatic position marvellously expressed in this shrunken body. The beardless, bony face reflects his profound feeling. His outward excitment has passed on to his lion which roars but watches his master in complete obedience. The surroundings are perfectly in keeping with the nature of the picture. Like most of the works of Leonardo da Vinci, this one is more a sketch than a finished work, a mere outline. It is the only authentic original by the master in Rome. Its conception is very original with its brown on brown colour scheme.

THE DEAD CHRIST. — This picture by Giov. Bellini (1430-1516) is a masterpiece also attributed to Mantegna and to Bartolomaeus Montagna. Mary Magdalene, Nicodemus and Joseph of Arimathea gravely prepare the body of Christ for burial. One of the men is gently holding the corpse in a sitting position. The pale face, the open mouth and the closed eyes reflect the former, heavy struggle until the final «It is consummated». The other manly figure, greatly heightened, has a serious expression on his bearded face and holds a vase from which The Kneeling Mary Magdalene takes the ointment to heal the wound on one of His hands. Her expression is also one of gentle, restrained grief.

ST. HELENA. — With great reserve and no attempt at ostentation, this painting by Paolo Veronese (1528-1588) exercises a peculiar effect upon us. It permits us to see into the interior vision of the empress. The face with its profound repose, completely absorbed by its interior vision, harmonizes wonderfully in its grey paleness with the famous silver-grey of the artist. The heavy, ceremonial dress is painted with the utmost technical finish. He'ena, the mother of Constantine, found the Holy Cross while on her way to Jerusalem.

THE CORONATION OF THE VIRGIN. — The first great picture by Raffael, from the year 1503. Over the Apostles, who are gathered in admiration round the coffin, the Virgin, surrounded by angels, is being crowned by her Son. The sweet adoration of the Virgin among youthful beauty, by the admiring old men, is a masterpiece of an artist not yet twenty years old. It is divided into two halves, each being a picture in itself. The youthful features and marvellous purity of expression and gesture are quite admirable.

THE PINACOTHECA VATICANA. — On the left is «The Visitation» by Raffael, — his last and unfinished work. The lower part was completed by his pupils. In the centre is Raffael's famous «Madona di Foligno» and on the right, «The Communion of St. Jerome» by Domenichino, one of the most famous pieces of the whole Vatican Collection.

ST. ROMUALD'S DREAM. — A. Sacchi (1600-1661) painted this admirable picture which in the olden days was so much admired that it was reckoned among the seven best pictures in Rome. It is remarkable for the unity of the whole in composition, presentation and colouring. St. Romuald is recounting his dream to his companions.

ST. MATTHEW. — By Guido Reni (1575-1642). The angel looks up to the old saint confidently and with love. The apostle, with every line of his careworn face en-nobled by divine inspiration, attentively watches the mouth of the Heavenly Messenger and quickly takes down his message. The angel uses his finger to explain his mission more clearly.

THE MARRIAGE OF ST. CATHERINE. — Murillo has painted the Virgin and
the saints on numerous occasions with Spanish magnificence of colour. St. Catherine here
is a beautiful Andalusian peasant and only her eyes and her absorbed expression betray
her special vocation to be married to the Lord. The picture was given to Pope Pius IX
by Elizabeth II of Spain.

«THE ADORATION OF THE SHEPHERDS» BY MURILLO. — Few painters have painted the Virgin as many times as Murillo. No other Spanish painter managed to present her image with so much naturalness. Here we see her as a Sevilian mother with her child, while the foster father is clearly also Andalusian. The Mother and Child are surrounded by a celestial light. which outshines the daylight of the landscape and illumines also the amazed, bewildered and most human shepherds. A typical Murillo.

THE MARTYRDOM OF ST. LAWRENCE BY G. RIBERA, «IL SPAGNOLET-
TO». — The Italians called this painter «The Little Spaniard». From the year 1616 he
was court painter at Naples and drew his typical figures from the rough, dock-side people
such as these here martyring, the saint who has surrendered himself completely in the
surety of his eternal life. As often in the paintings of Ribera, the cruel aspect of the
martyrdom is reflected in this picture.

THE DOGE NICCOLO MARCELLO. — A youthful work of Titian (1477-1576).
Perfect in characterisation and execution this is an excellent example of the famous golden
tones of the master.

THE TABERNACLE OF CARDINAL STEFANESCHI. — Giotto created this marvellous altar with the help of his pupils about 1300. In the centre is the enthroned Lord, surrounded by angels and worshipped by the donor. On the right, the crucifixion of St. Peter. His naked body is treated with surprising understanding and presented in a manner typical of Giotto's dramatic power. On the left, the beheading of St. Paul. The women on either side are treated in a very realistic way. The back of the altar is also painted. In the centre is St. Peter between angels, worshipped by cardinal Stefaneschi and another bishop a rare theme. The dignity of St. Peter and the nobility of position and expression of the angels is very forceful. On either side are Andrew and John, James and Paul.

ST. PETER FISHING. — This is one of the most beautiful tapestries of the Vatican collections. In the two small boats are six great figures with a peculiar enchantment about them. The figures are beautifully, lithe and have a most natural liveliness. In the first boat the men are busy with the overflowing net; in the other St. Peter is kneeling before the Lord with an earnest expression of devotion.: «Depart from me, My Lord, I am a sinful man!» But Jesus answers: «Do not fear! From now on you will be a fisher of men.» In the margin below, Cardinal Leo X entering the conclave in 1513.

SALA A CROCE GRAECA. — At the entrance are two sphinxes, both of Roman workmanship. On the left is the porphyry sarcophagus of Constantina, daughter of Constantine, the Great. (4th. cent. A. D.) Opposite is a similar sarcophagus of her mother, St. Helena. The decoration on both is typical of the period. In the centre of the room is a mosaic from the 3rd. cent. A. D., representing the various phases of the moon.

THE SALA ROTUNDA. — A rotunda with cupola built in the 18th. Cent. by Simonetti in the style of the Pantheon. Ten great niches form the circle. In eight are statues and the other two serve as a passage. On the floor are marvellously preserved mosaics of the Ist. cent. A. D. representing scenes from the battles between Greeks and centaurs and tritons who carry pretty young Nereids on their tails. The head of Medusa in the centre is modern. The porphyry bowl is made out of one piece and is of the 2nd. Cent. A. D. It was probably from the Roman Forum. This is a noble room which greatly impresses the visitor and appears to be made specially for the exposition of antiquities.

ZEUS OTRICOLI. — Sala Rotunda. This head must be imagined upon a colossal, enthroned statue the god, leaning forward slightly and looking upon his worshippers with a fine, inscrutable smile giving consolation. The features speak of an interior exaltation notwithstanding the the apparent calm. The eyes are deeply set. The lips are mild and majestical like no human mouth. The godlike power seems to flow from the hair and beard. This famous original was a work of the young Attic school of the 4th. Cent. B. C. Goethe had a copy in his room in Rome «before which he prayed every morning».

SERAPIS. — Sala Rotunda. Pluro or Hades, the brother of Zeus, with a bushe on his head. The master of the Underworld has a stern, bard expression and his eyes have none of the affection of his brother's. They seem to be very distant. He has been given various significations, among others that of the god of the sun. As Osiris he lighted the living during the day and the dead at night. Osiris and Apis are united in the figure of Serapis. Supposed copy of Greek original by Bryaxis from 4th. cent. B. C.

HERCULES. — Sala Rotunda. Gilded bronze statue. The body of this mighty hero of antiquity looms up most impressively. He stands with great self-assurance, his right hand resting on a club, the left holding the lion's skin from which he has derived his terrific strength. He has a far away look in his eye. This statue was excavated in 1864, being with its twelve feet of height, the biggest known bronze statue of antiquity. The original of this freely conceived copy belongs to the 4th. cent. B. C.

HERA. — Sala Rotunda. Before us rises the great goddess, queen and mistress, but her head is lowered in a humble attitude which seems to promise the fulfillment of supplications. Like Aphorodite, she wears the thin Greek clothing which reveals the human form beneath and only the lower part of the body is clad in the thick, heavy mantle which gives it a severe, solemn dignity. Roman copy after a work by the school of Phydias, called after the first owner, Hera Barberina.

ANTINOUS AS BACCHUS. — Sala Rotunda. The beautiful youth from Bythinia, the favourite of the Emperor Hadrian, died voluntarily in order to prolong the life of the emperor. (130 A. D.) He is represented with an ivy crown, large eyes, a full mouth, thick neck, and large, well-arched breast.

The expression even in its youthfulness has something mysterious about it, bad and cruel. The original drapery in bronze was restored in marble by Thorwaldsen. This colossal statue of Roman art of the 2nd cent. A. D. was found at the villa Hadrianus.

SEA-GOD PERSONIFIED AS THE GULF OF BAEJA. — Sala Rotunda. The enormous head seems to be streaming with hair and beard, the wet lower part lying flattened on the breast, which seems to have an overall leaf pattern made out of waves. The head is crowned with vineleaves. The features are gentle and sad. The small horns and the two dolphins in his beard give an indication of the dimensions of this enormous bust. Roman copy of Greek original of 2nd. cent. B.C.

SALA DELLE MUSE. — An octogonal room by Simonetti to unite the Sala Rotunda with the Sala degli Animali. The mural paintings are by Conca. In the centre of the cupola is the victory of Apollo over Marsyas. On the sixteen columns are antique capitals from the Villa Hadrianus. On the floor antique mosaics and in the centre a head of Medusa with arabesques from the 2nd. cent. A.D. Amidst the muses, their chief, Apollo, in a festive robe flying the the breeze, si accompanying himself on the cithara. His head is bowed as if he were dreaming and he opens the dance. Roman copy of famous bronze by Praxiteles of the 4th. cent. B.C.

EUTERPE. — A lovely girl with a flute in her hand sitting on a rock. The origin of this much restored statue is uncertain, the head belonging to another figure. Seven muses were found at Tivoli in 1774 together with the Apollo Musagetes. All Roman copies after Greek bronzes of th 4th. cent. B.C. To complete the number of muses, Urania, a Roman copy of a Greek original of the 4th. cent. and Euterpe, a Roman copy of a Geek original of the 3rd, cent. B.C., were added to the rest.

DANCE OF THE CORYBANTES. — Sala delle Muse. The Greeks considered
the dance of arms as the most important training for the battle. We see here two pairs
of naked youths opposite each other, covered only with shields, and the right foot
advanced. The right hand is armed with a sword which each one tries to plunge in his
adversary's breast as soon as he exposes himself. Imitation of an Attic relief of the 4th.
cent. B.C.

BIRTH OF DIONYSIUS. — Sala delle Muse. When Semele was struck by lightening, Zeus took the six months old fruit from the mother's womb and put it in his hip
until it completed its maturation. The little Dionysius comes out of Zeus hip, rising to the
arms of Hermes who holds a panther's skin ready to envelope him. On the right the
three Hores, who will occupy themselves with his education, are preparing a feast. By the
simplest means a continuous story is narrowed down, cutting out all unnecessary detail of
persons and things. Copy of Greek original of 5 th. cent. B. C.

ΠΕΡΙΚΛΗΣ
ΞΑΝΘΙΠΠΟΥ

PERICLES. — Sala delle Muse. Pericles regarded authoritative Democracy as the
best form of Government. We see him with his helmet, a token of his rank as chief of
the army. The noble, simple features reveal an inner strength and serenity with which
he was able to guide the unruly and hostile mass of the people even moments of great
difficulty. It is the image of a wise, earnest man, a born leader who knew not only how
to gain peace, but also how to preserve it for his people. Replica of a bronze bust by
Cresilas which was exposed in the Acropolis in the 4th. Cent. B.C. in Pericles own life-time.

PLATO. — Sala delle Muse. Plato came from a very noble family. His associa-
tion with Socrates was to be decisive in his spiritual evolution. This higly gifted poet and
philosopher developed his talents in the course of extensive travels and in 387 B. C., at the
age of forty, he returned to Athens and founded his famous Academy. His writings
have been passed down to us complete. The mighty head and the expression on the
strong, noble face give the impression of a completely self-sufficient man. The hair and
beard are designed in the same way to underline the unity of the head. The inscription
«Zenon» is false. Roman copy after Greek original from 4 th. cent. B. C.

SALA DEGLI ANIMALI. — The octagonal room is supported by four granite columns. The greater part of the individual statues and the groups are modern or restored. by F. A. Franzoni (1734-1818) after remains of old pieces. — 83 Ethiopian ram from the Villa Medici. — 143. The Rape of Europa, very much restored. 139 Hercules carrying off the Nemean lion. — 131 Hercules killing the Thracian Diomedes. — 127 Centaur bearing a cupid on his back. — 126 Commodus on horseback. A very rare representation which served Bernini for his Constantine the Great at S. Peter's. Roman from 3rd. cent. A.D. 13a. Slaughtered ram unpon the altar as a sacrifice.

MOLOSSER DOG. — Sala degli Animali. In the Cortile de Belvedere, at the entrance of the Sala degli Animali are the two Molosser Dogs. These dogs of the Sicilian Attic race were very much used for hunting in ancient times. Replica of a hellenic original of the 3rd. cent. B.C. 151. Relief. Love in a biga with two wild boars as a symbol that he is able to subject even the most ferocious 202. Colossal head of a camel after a hellenic original from the 2nd. cent. B.C., 38 Hercules killing Geryoneus. 42 Hercules with Cerberus. 49,56 Peacocks, the symbol of eternity, from the tomb of Emperor Hadrian. 158 Two greyhounds playing. 62 Triton stealing a Nereid to whose assistance cupids come running. Perhaps a Greek original from the 2nd. cent. B. C. from a water pipe in front of the Porta Latina. 68 Torso of Minotaur. Copy a Greek original of the 5th. cent. B. C.

MELEAGER. — Sala degli Animali. The King of Calydon once forgot to sacrifice to Artemis, and the offended goddess sent the Calydonian Boar to lay waste the land. Many heroes came to kill the beast, among them Atalanta, the daughter of the king of Tegea. Meleager, the son of the king of Calydon, killed the beast and gave the trophies to his beloved Atalanta. A fight started about the dead animal in which Meleager killed his mother's brothers. To avenge them, his mother burnt a piece of wood upon which his life depended according to an old prophecy. With the burning of the wood his life faded away. Copy of famous bronze by Scopas of 4th. cent. B.C.

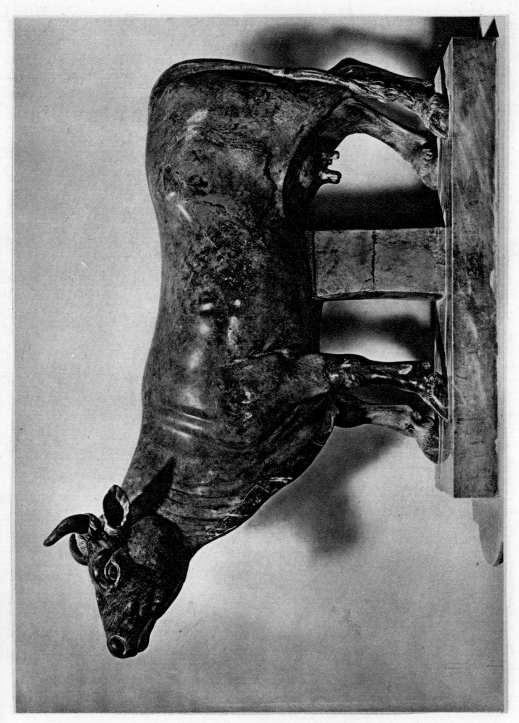

MYRON'S COW. — Sala degli Animali. It is doubtful if this grey marble cow is a true copy of that by Myron in bronze which made the artist so famous. The Greek historians tell us that this was so realistic that it was always being mistaken for a real cow. A lion wanted to kill it, a steer wanted to leap upon it, a calf to drink from it. A shepherd threw a stone at it and struck it; a peasant brought a yoke and plough to plough with it; a thief tried to steal it, a fly to bite it, and even Myron confused it with his own cows.

A RITUAL IMAGE FROM A TEMPLE OF MITHRA. — Sala degli Animali.
The steer was the first creature created by Ahuramazda, the god of light. Its death
signifies the origin of all creation. The god of the sun, with Phrygian bonnet, kills the
beast with his knife. The snake which is drinking the blood is the symbol of the earth
which is fertilised by this liquid. The scorpion eating up its genital organs personifies
evil destroying the power of creation. The dog springing upon the wound is to receive
the soul and bring it to its new destination. Roman from 2nd. cent. A. D.

VIEW FROM THE GALLERIA DELLE STATUE INTO THE SALA DEI BUSTI. — Built between 1484 and 1492 by Pollajuolo and decorated with famous mural paintings by Pinturicchio and Mantegna. Later restored by Pope Clement XIV, it was considerably enlarged by Pope Pius VI, the wallpaintings being destroyed all but a few remains in the lunettes. In the background is the famous Zeus Verospi with the thunder in his right hand. This is a copy of a hellenic original of the 3rd. cent., B. C. Right and left are the sitting statues of the comedians Menander (died 290 B. C.) and Posidippius, who lived about 265 B. C., both are replicas of Greek bronze statues of the 3rd. cent. B. C.

APOLLO SAUROCTONOS. — Galleria delle Statue. The young god represented as a beautiful youth on the threshold of manhood, leaning against a tree, awaiting the lizard which is crawling up it. In his right hand he holds the dart with which he is going to kill it, hence the name which means «Lizard Killer». The beautifully moulded, youthful body, the exquisite, almost feminine features and the movement conveyed in the static figure are truly marvellous. Copy of bronze figure by Praxiteles, excavated in 1777 at the Palatinus.

EROS OF CENTOCELLE. — Galleria delle Statue. Eros, the son of Zeus, was the go-between of Olympus and Earth. Formerly called «The Genius of the Vatican», this statue may represent a spirit of death which has become changed to Eros. The small head with the tangled curls seems to have a melancholy expression. Under puckered brows he sends a pleading look towards the object of his love. This expression alone can explain the great effect of this torso, «the dreamy melancholy of young love, deriving here from the very god of love himself». Replica of an original in bronze by the school of Praxiteles.

SLEEPING ARIADNE. — Galleria delle Statue. This work will always hold a leading place in art as a picture of tranquility. No lovely gracious woman could rest with greater majesty. Copy of Greek original of 3rd. cent. B.C.

AMAZON. — Galleria delle Statue. The most beautiful Amazon of Rome from the Villa Mattei. According to a cameo design, she holds a spear in both hands, the left under, and the right over, the head. The spurleather on her left foot indicates that she is an amazon. The harmony of the body the striking contrast of movement and the artistry of the drapery distinguish this beautiful work which Nero is said always to have taken with him. The head is from another statue. Copy of a bronze by Cresylas of the 5th. cent. B. C.

VATICAN DANAIDE. — Galleria delle Statue. By order of their father, Danaos. king of Argos, the Danaides assassinated their husbands on their wedding night, They were therefore condemned in the Underworld to bring water in an perforated bowl, a symbol of never-ending, useles work. The gracious young creature holds the basin, leaning forward with a natural ease. The soft movement which animates neck, back waist and hips continuing down into the drapery is without equal. The figure may have been from a fountain. Copy from Greek original of 4th. cent. B. C.

PENELOPE. — Galleria delle Statue. Sadness seems to exude from the hopeless position and the sorrowful face of this woman abandoned to her grief. The dishevelled hair indicates the mourner's indifference to the outer world. This statue was made after an Attic original from the 5th. cent. B. C. which probably belonged to a tomb.

GROUP OF NIOBIDES. — Galleria delle Statue. The wounded young woman leans
dying against her flying brother, of whom only a part of his left side and his mantle are
visible. An incomparably beautiful and vivid work often called «Cephalus and Procris».
The head is ancient from another statue of the 3rd. cent. B. C.

DRUNKEN SATYR. — The satyr's love of wine here finds its best expression. He leans back, the right arm wantonly raised and the left on the wine-skin ready to take another swill. The curious position of the drunkard's body is animated by the line from the raised arm to the foot firmly placed to the ground. Copy of hellenic original of the 3rd. cent. B. C.

TRITON. — Galleria delle Statue. The Tritons, sons of Poseidon, have satyrs' ears, the centaurs' horse-like feet and fish tails. Their attribute is a pierced shell on which they blow softly or strongly according as they want to calm or disturb the waves. The face is somewhat agitated, the eyes deep-set, the eyebrows sharply arched, the beautiful mouth open and quivering, the forehead wrinkled. It was thus that the Greeks pictured the sea. In this being we see a torso in ancient form.

CRONOS. — Sala dei Busti. Cronos or Saturnus, father of Zeus, ate up all his children, it having been predicted that he would be killed by them. Only Zeus was saved by a trick. The rarely represented god is here shown as an old man. Fragment of a copy of a Greek original of the 4th. cent. B. C.

EMPEROR CARACALLA. — Sala dei Busti. A terrible head. An enemy of God and men whose malignity and treachery reminds one of Satan. With this head Roman art seems to come to an end, as if paralysed by fear. Since then nothing with great feeling for life was created (Burckhardt). Caralla governed from 211 to 217 A.D. This bust was found near the Basilica of Constantine.

MENELAUS. — Sala dei Busti. Menelaus, leader of the army at Troy, tries to save his dying friend Patroclus, in the midst of battle. The mighty head is greatly moved, the forehead wrinkled, the eyes tragic and the mouth wide-open as if about to utter a cry. All this is a demonstration of great fear for his friend — a noble image of friendship. Replica of a Greek original of the 4th. cent. B. C. Also called «Ajax with the dead Achilles». Compare the so-called Pasquino group on the west-corner of the Palazzo Braschi at Rome.

PORTRAIT OF THE ROMAN COUPLE. — Sala dei Busti. Man and wife, also called «Cato and Portia». The visible difference of age may lead one to believe that they are father and daughter. Both characters are marvellously portrayed. The woman simple and homely, a loving and dutiful wife; the man severe and pre-occupied as the head of the family and somewhat pedantic. This marvel of Roman sculpture dates from the Ist. cent. B.C. The German historian Niebuhr had a copy made for his tomb. at Bonn.

AUGUSTUS. — Sala dei Busti. The reserved, aristocratic manner finds its most perfect expression here. The beautiful, high forehead reveals intelligence, the firm mouth and chin — energy, and the shapely, slightly curved nose — hidden and controlled passion. The face is earnest, presaging future responsibility; the eyes have the calm of innate dignity. A happily conceived portrait of a youth who is every inch a born emperor. This bust is also called Octavius. Augustus lived 31. B. C., 14. A. D.

FOUR MOSAICS. — Gabinetto delle Maschere. Eight alabaster columns from Monte Circeo support the ceiling. On the floor are are four very fine mosaics of the 2nd. cent. A. D., found, in 1780, at the Villa Hadrianus near Tivoli. The left upper one represents the four masks of comedy. The one beneath it represents a dionysian mask with different symbols of that god. The upper right, a laurel-adorned one with symbols of Apollo. The fourth one represents an Olympic countryside. The rest is modern.

DANCER. — Gabinetto delle Maschere. A beautifully clad and beautifully moving figure with a head of dionysian sweetness which is ancient but later than the rest which a Roman copy of a Greek original of the 4th. cent. B. C. Goethe saw it in Naples. A few days before his return to Germany it was offered to him secretly for 300 pieces of gold. The husband of Angelica Kaufmann (Goethe's great love in Italy) advised him not to take it and so he abandoned it after have long thought over his «passionate love».

SATYR WITH GRAPES. — Gabinetto delle Maschere. The satyr looks at the
bunch of grapes with an expression of unashamed and loving hunger. The hellenistic
original of the 2nd. cent. B.C. must have been very famous because there are a very
great number of copies from it. It was found in the Villa Hadrianus and is made of a
reddish marble called Rosso Antico.

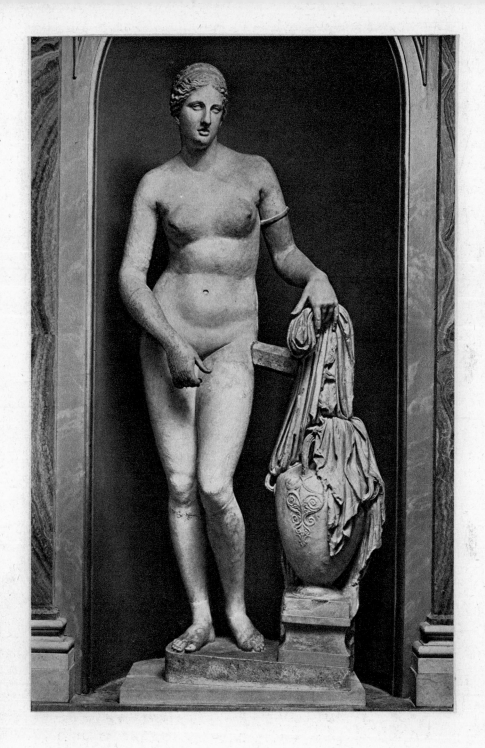

APHRODITE FROM KNIDOS. — Gabinetto delle Maschere. This statue is the best existing Greek copy of the Venus of Knidos by Praxiteles. The original head is at Berlin. The Greeks did not mind a long trip to see it. The original was destroyed during a fire. Aphrodite, preparing to bathe, lets her clothing fall unashamedly. Her expression is very lovely and her eyes have a look of passionate delight. The silky hair smoothly envelopes the small head and the full curves of the fine body are beautifully delineated.

KNEELING VENUS. — The goddess is kneeling under the water falling from a fountain. The difficulty of realizing the limbs in this position has been wonderfully worked out. The inscription «Bupalos» is modern from a base which was found on the statue. Very much restored Roman copy of a hellenic original of the 3rd. cent. B. C.

CORTILE DI BELVEDERE. — This famous courtyard was constructed by G. da Petrasanta after plans by Bramante, under Pope Innocent VIII (1484-1492). In the centre is a fountain and in the eight corners and the middle of each side, there are niches containing works of art. In 1775 this was changed by Simonetti who created the uninteresting corridor. Since the time of Pope Pius VI (1775-1799) this part of the Vatican Collection has been called the Museo Pio-Clementino. In 1803 Pope Pius VII had four pavilions constructed which were named after the four statues Laocoon, Apollo, Perseus and Hermes, which were then installed there. Over the eight arches are eight antique masks and over the columns, eight antique reliefs.

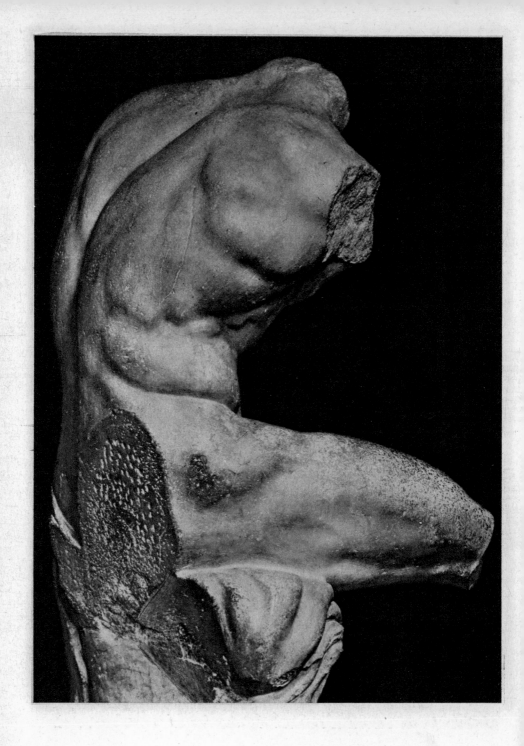

THE TORSO OF BELVEDERE. — From Michaelangelo to Winckelman, Goethe, and Burckhardt, the world famous torso has been considered as the highest achievement in existing art. According to the inscription it is by the Athenian Apollonius (Ist. cent. B. C.), but it may be a copy of a much older original. Every attempt at interpretation or reconstruction so far has been in vain. Goethe said of it that he was even prepared to consider it as the most beautiful thing he had ever seen.

APOLLO OF BELVEDERE. — There is hidden power in this lithe body which seems to follow the course of the arrow sent from his bow. As it reaches its target the god looks away with proud disdain.

LAOCOON. — Belvedere. Laocoon was a priest of Apollo at Troy. For a former
crime he is overwhelmed by two giant snakes. His youngest son is bitten in the side,
and his head falls back as he dies. The father defends himself with all his might as
the snake tries to bite him in a most sensitive part. The pain streaks like lightening
through his body, and with a cry he twists his head upon his neck. A whole world of
anguish, terror and despair are reflected in his features. This is one of the very few
Greek originals that have come down to us. 2nd. cent. B.C.

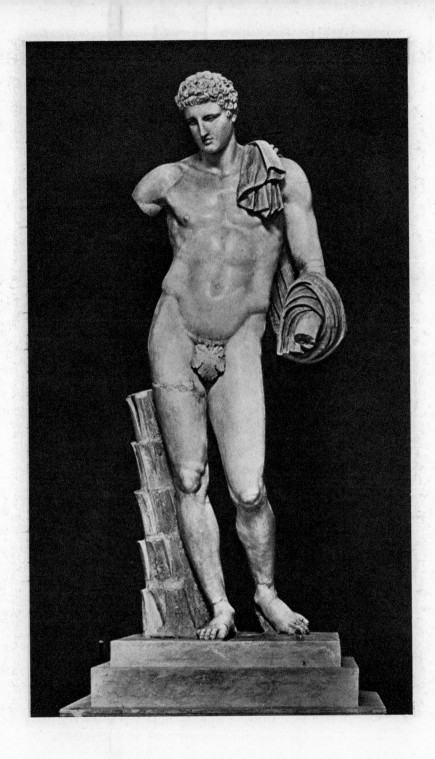

HERMES OF BELVEDERE. — Hermes, the son of Zeus and Maya, the messenger god was also the patron of gifted and skillful men, and the god of travel and voyages. As such he accompanied the dead from Olympus to the Underworld. Here he appears as the protector of Gymnasiums and a beautiful specimen of a well-proportioned human body. The bronze original of this most perfect of all statues of Hermes in Italy is of the 4th. cent. B.C.

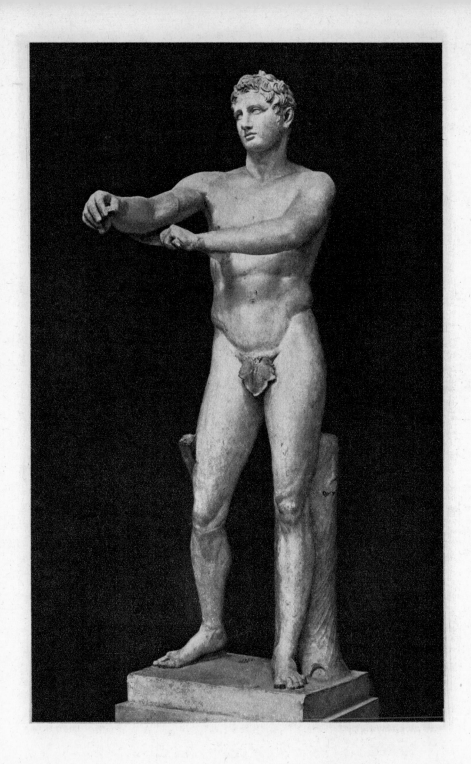

APOXYOMENOS. — Gabinetto del A. The Scraper. So called from his gesture
of cleaning himself after the arena with a scraper. The beautifully articulated body is
no weight for the legs whose slightly advanced position produces a really masterly line.
A marvellous copy from the famous bronze by Lysippo. The original was put up by
Agrippa in front of the Pantheon.

RELIEF OF BELVEDERE. — Apollo's Room. Two slaves of the temple are leading
a reluctant steer to the sacrifice. The flowing garments are wonderfully wrought. Antique marble, copy of a relief on the balustrade of the Acropolis. 5th. cent. B. C.

GABINETTO DI CANOVA. — Contains three masterpieces by this famous artist of Napoleon's time. In the centre is Perseus with the head of the Medusa Gorgo, and a copy of the Apollo Belvedere. On the left and right are the boxers Creugas and Damoxenes. The statues are cold and lifeless, and even though their executions is masterly, technically perfect and very elegant, they remain a vain attempt at the reproduction of the masterpieces of ancient times.

GIARDINA DELLA PIGNA. — Bramante constructed the fountain in the form of an arch of triumph. The courtyard has its name from the pineapple in gilded bronze, eight feet high, which in olden times decorated a fountain and gave its name to a whole district of the town. The water used to spout out of holes in the scales. Later the pineaple was put in the Atrium of the old Basilica of St. Peter's, where Dante saw it on the occasion of the first Holy Year in 1300 and mentioned it as «The Pineapple of St. Peter's» (Inf. XXXI 58). On either side are bronze peacocks from the tomb of Hadrian.

SALA DELLA BIGA (see page 187).

BEARDED DIONYSIUS. — Sala della Biga. Dionysius is the god of Nature. The broad figure is clad in a full robe, and the hair and beard are well-trimmed. The original was by Praxiteles. It is also known as «Sardanapolous».

DISCOBOLOS. — Sala delle Biga. According to the inscription the bronze original was by Myron, 5th. cent. B.C. The Vatican copy bears a modern head which is wrongly posed. The original had no tree. The artist has tried to capture the moment immediately before the throw. High speed photography could prove that the whole figure, the bent back, the movement of the arms, the position of the feet and every muscle corresponds exactly to reality, and the whole movement is in accordance with movement of a human body.

GALLERIA DEI CANDELABRI. — This collection got its name from the various pairs of candelabra exposed on either side of the arcades which divide the room. At the time of the foundation of the Museo Pio-Clementino, it was an open loggia which was closed in the time of Pius VI and put into its present form by Simonetti. The frescoes are by Dominico Torti and Ludwig Seitz, made under Pope Leo XIII (1883-1887). On the floor are fragments of ancient marbles from the Emporium.

SATYR WITH THE CHILD DIONYSIUS. — Galleria dei Candelabri. The young satyr steps lightly and suply, his lithe body seeming to be moved by seme inner inspiration, proud of his noble calling as the bearer of the little Dionysius. The lovely little boy on the satyr's shoulders, carries a bunch of grapes in his right hand and tries to clutch the cup with his left. Roman copy of Greek original of 3rd. cent. B. C.

RUNNER. — Galleria dei Candelabri. The Greeks also had girls running in races in honour of Hera, and this gave a new motif to artists. The slim body with its shapely legs is a lovely portrait of a young virgin. The short hair and short dress are typical of Greek athletics. The girl has won her race, hence the palm on the tree. Roman copy of Greek original from 5th. cent. B. C.

THE GOOSEKILLER. — Galleria dei Candelabri. Massive works which exalt all our being are well as public monuments. This sculpture, on the other hand, which even a child could delight in, seems more properly created for a private house, with its homely, intimate joy. The famous bronze original was by Boethos of Calcedonia. 2nd. cent. B.C.

GANYMEDE WITH THE EAGLE. — Galleria dei Candelabri. Antiquity had a famous bronze by Leochares: Ganymede taken up to heaven by the eagle. Pliny praised that statue and the way in which the eagle seems to know what he is stealing and for whom (Zeus), and being careful not to hurt the boy through his clothing. Here is another theme. The raising up of a human body most artistically realised as eagle, boy and dog gaze up to Zeus. The original of this is a very much restored copy of the 4th. cent. B.C.

TYCHE OF ANTIOCH. — Galleria dei Candelabri. The beautiful goddess of the
town of Antioch is sitting on a rock, surveying the land. The river god, Oronthes, the
greatest Syrian stream, comes up from the depths and she puts her foot on his. neck.
The fruits in her hand signify the fruitfulness of the earth. The original, from the
4th. cent. was at Antioch. There are very few works of antiquity which may compare
with this in the loveliness of the whole composition.

SARCOPHAGUS OF THE NIOBIDES. — Galleria dei Candelabri. Niobe, the wife of the king of Thebes, forbade festivals in honour of the goddess Leto, she having borne 14 children and Leto only 2. To avenge this insult to their mother, Apollo and Artemis killed the seven sons and seven daughters of Niobe. On the friese the dead Niobides are again depicted in artistic grouping. Roman of the 2nd. cent. A.D.

FOUNTAIN WITH THREE KNEELING SILENS. — Galleria dei Candelabri.
These are the ever-thirsty silens, proverbial for their sinfulness and slowness. Their
winesacks have been used to support the waterbasin. Imitation of a fountain at Athens.

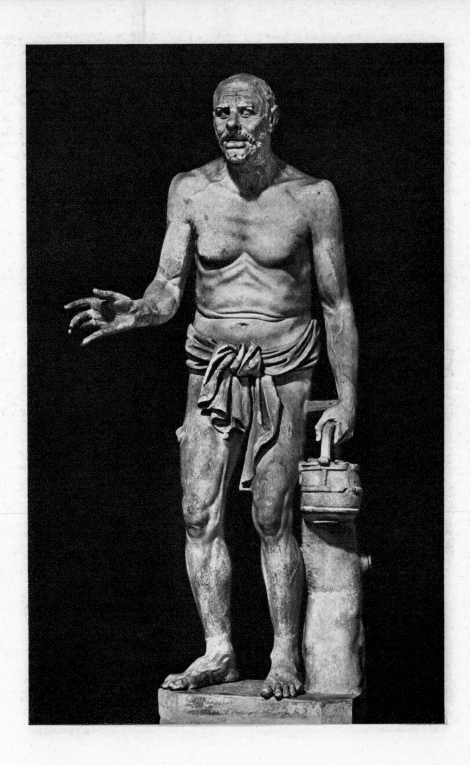

OLD FISHERMAN. — Galleria dei Candelabri. A picture of misery. Hard work has bent the old man. His knees shake and the body is thin. The indescribable expression on the face dominates the whole figure. The original of this seemingly modern work, so realistically conceived, dates from the 3rd. cent. B.C. and has no support. It has often been called «Old slave of the bath with a waterpot».

PAN DRAWING A THORN FROM THE FOOT OF A SATYR. — Galleria
dei Candelabri. The expression of long-suffering in the face of the satyr is magnificent.
He leans against a winesack from which the precious liquor runs. With his right hand
he holds up the paining foot which is studied with almost comic seriousness by Pan.
The combination of human and animal features and the way in which the human body
merges into the goat feet is excellently portrayed. Fountain at Villa Mattei. Roman
copy after an original of the 2nd. cent. B. C.

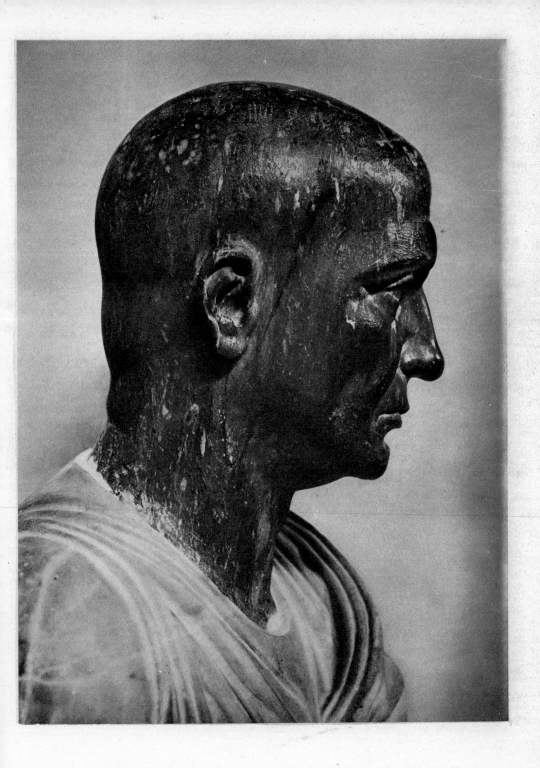

SO-CALLED SCIPIO. — Galleria Chiaramonti. Portrait of a priest of Isis. The shorn head and the small crucifix on his forehead indicate his priestly calling. A magnificent portrait of a Roman from the beginning of the Ist. cent. A.D. Nero antique marble on a white bust.

NIOBE. — Galleria Chiaramonti. The daughter of Niobe flying from the wrath of Apollo. Even without being able to observe the expression of face and hands, we can imagine the agony of mind as she flees with cloak flying in the breeze. The original of this unique copy was, perhaps, by Scopas, and stood in 35 B. C. before the Capitol in Rome.

DANCING GODDESSES. — Galleria Chiaramonti. This perfect central figure and the one to its right are found in the Vatican. Of the third figure only an arm and a cup remain. This represents the Hores, the goddesses who bring fruit and flowers during the year, dancing at a feast The windswept robes are beautifully executed. In spite of the simplicity it is artistically perfect. A jewel of the Vatican collection. Attic relief of the 5th. cent. B. C.

RIDER OF BOETHIA. — Galleria Chiaramonti. The plaque is from ta tomb, a
Greek original in the style of Phidias of the 5th. cent. B. C. The rider portrait has
a certain similitude with the relief from the Parthenon but its proportions are greater.
The correct and natural position on horseback, the fine delineation of the muscles of the
arm culminating in the soft line of the wrist, are wrought with an intimate knowledge
of human anatomy. The head is also beautifully characterized.

DIONYSIUS. — Galleria Chiaramonti. There is a certain animal quality in the soft features of the face, the small moist eyes, the slightly open mouth. Nevertheless this is a noble being of great beauty. The head is finely shaped and the hair neatly rolled over a band. The shapeless bush of hair above reminds one of the bestial origins of the god. Copy of Greek original of the 4th. cent. B.C.

DIONYSIUS AND SATYR. — Galleria Chiaramonti. A famous group. Dionysius,
naked and with a wine cup in his hand and ivy and grapes in his hair is leaning on a
satyr. At his side is a panther. The contrast between the god and the satyr is striking.
The original was a famous piece of Greek art from the 4 th. cent. B. C.

HERACLES WITH TELEPHOS. — Galleria Chiaramonti. A most beautiful representation of the famous hero. The boy was the fruit of a secret love with Auge, a priestess of Athena. Herakles being absent, the outraged father of Auge exposed the child, but a hind looked after it until its father returned and found it. The two figures were combined at a later date. The original of Heracles is from 4th. cent. B.C. and the child from 3rd. cent. B.C.

ODYSSEUS. — Galleria Chiaramonti. Odysseus, detained as prisoner with his companions by the one-eyed Giant, Cyclops, hopes to make the ogre drunk in order to burn out his eye. The project succeeds and they get free. Here is Odysseus offering the wine. His position is dangerous because the giant may seize him instead of the wine. For this reason he goes cautiously, with outstretched hand and foot ready to fly at the slightest movement. The expression in the deep-set eyes is wonderfully wrought. Roman copy of Greek original of the 3rd. cent. B. C.

VILLA PIA IN THE VATICAN GARDENS. — In 1562 Pirro Ligorio erected this papal pavilion with a vestibilium, two separate entrances, fresh fountains and a symmetrical tower with a loggia, the whole made in the form of a terrace with stairs. The rich plastic, ornamentation of the façade harmonises with the surroundings. The Villa is decorated with statues, mosaics, pictures and terracottas. In former times the Popes used to receive ladies in audience here.

BRACCIO NUOVO (see page 190).

PUDICIZIA. — A famous clathed statue. The folds of the garments are beautifully depicted. The expression on the lovely face is enigmatic as also that of the right
hand. Probably a Mnemosyne, mother of the Muses. The erect bearing and the long
flowing robes emphasize the height of the figure. The original was of the 3rd. cent. B. C.

DIANA LUCIFERA. — Braccio Nuovo. Diana bearing a light is here a fullyclo-
thed, gentle virgin, similar to Aphrodite in the roundness and expression of the face.
The dress falls lightly over the beautiful body. The head is earlier. Roman copy of
Greek original of 4th. cent. B. C.

CARYATIDE. — Braccio Nuovo. A number of solemn and earnest Caryatide used
at one time to adorned the Erechtheion in place of the columns. As servants of the
goddess they bear the celling of the temple upon their cups. Their position is, however,
light and their lovely, perfect bodies are full of rhythmic grace. This face expresses a
virginal purity. Copy of Greek original of 5th. cent. B. C.

WOUNDED AMAZON. ⊢ Braccio Nuovo. She leans wearily against a pillar, her hand raised in anguish at the wound under her right breast. Her face betrays great pain. The bronze original by Polyclet was one of the fives amazons in the sanctuary of Artemis at Ephesus and was recognised to be better than that of Phidias. The three others were by Cresilas, Kydon and Phradmon. Judging by her position, the form of the body and the clothing, she belongs to the severe, elevated style of the 5th. cent., but the coming age of Praxiteles and Scopas with their greater freedom and beauty is already foreshadowed in this work. The arms and legs were restored by Thorwaldsen.

EURIPIDES. — Braccio Nuovo. This statue of a Greek poet, after an original of the 4th. cent. B.C. was restored in the time of Pope Pius VII with the head of Euripides. The mouth expresses fine and bitter irony. The eyes are bent to the ground, and deepset. Euripides, born 480 B.C. was one of the greatest tragedians of the Greeks. Of his 92 tragedies only a few have come down to us. The Athenians effected a bronze statue to him and put it in the theatre with those of Sophocles and Aeschylus.

DEMOSTHENES. — Braccio Nuovo. The greatest orator of Greece, whose aim was the liberty and glorification of Athens. He incited resistance to Philip of Macedon and, having lost his fatherland, he committed suicide. The statue is simple and unornate, dominated by the force of the personality which is revealed in the face. The impediment in his speech is clearly seen in the formation of the mouth.

ASCLEPIUS. — Braccio Nuovo. The son of Apollo and Coronis was killed by Zeus who feared that men could be protected by him against death. Here he is supposed to be resting between two visits to the sick, but even now his energetic spirit shines forth. This is a youthful Asclepius, with the features of Musa, Augustus' doctor. Roman copy of Greek original of 4th. cent. B.C.

RESTING SATYR. — Braccio Nuovo. One of the most imitated themes of ancient art, of which many museums possess copies. The resting satyr, leaning against a
tree, with a crown on his head and a skin on his shoulder. The whole figure and especially the face reflect a love of nature. The animal desire of these creatures as represented in the old statues, is here refined into a roguish sensuality. Leaning against a
tree, the figure gives an impression of resting lightly and easily on its feet. Copy of
famous statue by Praxiteles.

MINERVA GIUSTINIANA. — Braccio Nuovo. Here the Greek style has found
its most ideal expression. There is an assuring strength revelled in the clear cut features.
At her feet is the sacred snake, the symbol of her domination over Athens. Copy of
a bronze of the 4th. cent. B.C.

AUGUSTUS. — Braccio Nuovo. In the flower of his manhood, the founder of his empire is represented as emperor, as illustrated in the armour and the naked feet which betoken a hero. The beautifully wrought relief work on the cuirass represents his legends and episodes from his victorious campaign against the Parthes. In the centre are two captives personifying, the subjugated Spain on the left, and Gaul on the right. The statue is a masterpiece among Roman portraits and was made at about the turn of the century.

DORYPHOROS. — Braccio Nuovo. As winner of the game, the youth may erect his statue. The body in repose clearly exhibits its prowess in the sharply defined muscles under the skin, the whole forming a harmonious unity. The famous bronze statue by Polycletus, «The Spear Bearer» has been copied innumerable times and has become a standard with its perfect proportions. Lysipius called it «his master».

THE RIVER NILE. — Braccio Nuovo. The mighty, sprawling figure characterises
the slow running, majestic river. The Sphinx, crocodile and ichneumon signify signify
Egypt. The sixteen spirits are the sixteen ells that the river must rise to flood the
country. The face expresses the quiet contentment of the benefactor as he gazes into
the distance. The figure was excavated in 1513 at St. Mary sopra Minerva. It is a copy
from an original of the 2nd. cent. B. C.

VIEW OF THE ETRUSCAN MUSEUM. — This collection was founded in 1836 by Pope Gregory XVI. It is almost entirely composed of pieces found the the excavations in the necropolis of western Etruria, especially near Vulci. There is an astonishing amount of bronzes, sarcophagi, terracottas and famous vases. On the left is the well-known statue of Mars of Todi, a technically perfect but uninspiring work of early Italo-Greek art of the 4th. cent. B.C. The bronze biga, or chariot, the decorations of whose wheels are remarkably well conserved, is of the 5th. or 4th. cent. B.C. The wood-work is imitation.

VASE BY EXEKIAS. — Museo Etrusco. Achilles and Ajax gambling during a respite in the fighting. The numbers four and three signify that Achilles has four good points and his friend remains one point behind him as always. On the other side are Castor and Pollux being joyfully received by their parents Leda and Tindar. The perfect silhouettes, lovely proportions and soft, graphite ornamentation make this vase the most perfect specimen of ceramic of the second half of the sixth cent. B. C. The bare spaces are convered with inscriptions by the artist, Exekias, the famous vase-painter of Athens.

ETRUSCAN ORNAMENTS. — Museo Etrusco Gregoriana. These precious, artistic pieces are from the famous tomb Regolini-Galassi at Cerveteri, an Etruscan tomb. They date from the 7th. cent. B. C., but in spite of the very early period, these objects are notable in the masterly technique of the proportions and line. It is understandable that even the Greeks imported such articles from the Etruscan workshops.

BASALT LION. — Museo Egiziano. Two lions, exactly alike, face each other upon quadrangular foundations with hieroglyphic inscriptions telling of the rule of the last king of the XXXth. dynasty — Nectanebo II ((378-361, B.C.). Originally intended by this king for his tomb, they used to stand in front of a temple, and after the conquest of Egypt they were brought to Rome. Goethe already remarked on them as rare pieces of art. These huge, grandiose figures symbolize the a divine power of Nature in Egypt. They are from the 4th. cent. B. C.

QUEEN TUAA. — Museo Egiziano. This colossal statue of the mother of Ramses II, from about 1280 B.C. is of black granite. The precision and craftsmanship with which this figure has been wrought out of the brittle stone and then polished, is truly remarkable. The body and face are firm and hard. In her right hand she holds the princess Hont-Ma-ra. Her name is engraved on her crown. On the back there are hieroglyphics.

NAOPHORE. — Museo Egiziano. The basalt statue of king Utahor-resent-pan holding a small shrine. The statue is old, but the head is modern. The hieroglyphics on the clothes tell that he was a priest of the goddess Neit at Sais and that this town was destroyed in 525 B.C. by the Persian king Kambyses. The famous text gives an extract of Egyptian history of the 6th. cent. B.C.

CANOPO. — Museo Egipziano. The head of this very famous alabaster vase is
one of the best representations of the Alexandrine god Canopo. The vase, which is of
the 2nd. cent. A. D. was found at the Villa Tiburtiana, Hadrian's villa near Tivoli.

KING MENTUHOTEP IV. — Museo Egiziano. The head is covered with a tall cap containing hieroglyphic inscriptions. The youthful face with its fine, regular features has a strange, enigmatic smile playing round the mouth. In spite of its tremendous age (over four thousand years), there is something quite modern in the expression. This is the oldest portrait bist in the Vatican collection and is of sandstone.

RAFFAEL'S STANZES

The Stanzes, constructed in the time of Pope Nicholas V, were chosen by Pope Julian II for his home. In 1508 Raffael received orders to paint the four rooms. They are his masterpiece.

He began with the Stanza della Segnatura. The wall-paintings of this room are the most wonderful ones. Raffael himself finished this immense piece of work within two and a half years. For every fresco on the wall there is a corresponding one on the ceiling. Over the «Disputa» is the «Theologia», over the «Parnassus» the «Poesia»; «Philosophia» is over the School of Athens and «Justice» sits over the Cardinal Virtues of Prudence, Fortitude and Temperance. In the corners are «The First Sin», «Apollo, and Mars», «The Judgement of Solomon» and «Astronomia». At the base some paintings by Perino del Vaga.

From 1512-1514, Raffael painted the Stanza d'Eliodoro. The themes were also proposed by Julian II. On the main wall «The expulsion of Heliodorus», and over it en the ceiling «Moses before the Burning Bush», one of the most beautiful paintings of the master in the style of Michaelangelo. On the right the «Mass of Bolsena» with the «Sacrifice of Abraham» above. Next to it «The expulsion of Attila by Pope Leo I». The leader of the Huns is panic-stricken at the apparition of Peter and Paul who descend from heaven in the midst of a shining light. Next to this is «The Liberation of Peter» and over it, «The Jacob's Dream».

The Stanze del Incendio. Of these paintings executed between 1514 and 1517, there is probably only one by Raffael himself, — «The Fire in the Borgo». The rest are from sketches by Raffael, executed by his pupils, while the paintings on the ceiling are by Prugino. In the «Coronation of Charles the Great by Pope Leo III in 800», Leo III has the features of Leo X and the Emperor those of Francis I of France, — a remembrance of their meeting at Bologna in 1515. At the base «Charles the Great». Next to it is the «Victory of Pope Leo IV over the Saracens at Ostia in 849». Next comes «Pope Leo III exonerating himself on oath to Charles the Great against the acusations of his nephew, Pope Hadrian IV, at St. Peter's». An inscription at the base recalls that the oath proved useless when a divine voice reminded them that «only God may judge the bishops and no man is permitted to do so».

After the death of the master, the Sala di Constantino was finished by his pupils Romano and Penni, partly from sketches of Raffael, as, for instance, «The Victory of Constantine over Maxentius at Ponte Molle». This is the masterpiece of all battle pictures. Next to it is «Constantine's Speech to his troops after the Apparition of he Cross». Next comes «The Baptism of Constantine and his son by Pope Silvester». The last picture is «The gift of Rome to the Pope by Constantine at the old Basilica». The paintings on the ceiling are of a much later date.

RAFFAEL'S LOGGIAS

The three-floored Loggias, surrounded the Cortile di San Damaso, and were begun in 1512. by Bramante. Those of Raffael are on the second floor and were painted for Pope Leo X. These consist of an open corridor leading to the Stanzes, sub-divided into 13 small loggias with cupolas which are decorated with four rectangular wall-paintings each. In the four corners of the 13 cupolas, Raffael has represented his famous Bible scenes, 48 from the Old Testament and 4 from the New Testament. The designs were all his and the Eve of «The First Sin» is considered to be entirely done by him. The representations presented against a harmonious landscape, are so simple and so very human that he seems to be telling the Bible story to children.

The 52 pictures are: I. God divides light and darkness; God divides earth and water; God creates sun and moon, and God creates the animals. II. The creation of Eve, the first sin, the expulsion from the Garden of Eden, and Adam and Eve working. III. The construction of the ark, the Deluge, the abandonment of the ark and the thanksgiving of Noah. IV. Abraham and Melchisedek, God's promise to Abraham, the apparition of the three angels, Lot flying from Sodom. V. God appearing to Isaac, Abimelech listening to Isaac and Rebecca, Jacob and Rachel at the fountain and Esau asking for a blessing. VI. Jacob's dream, Jacob blessed by Isaac, Jacob demanding Rachel as wife and Jacob's return to Canaan. VII. Joseph narrating his dream to his brothers, Joseph sold by his brothers, Joseph and Potiphar's wife and Joseph before Pharoah. VIII. The finding of Moses, Moses in the burning bush, the crossing of the Red Sea and Moses extracting water from the stone. IX. Moses receiving the Commandments, the Adoration of the Golden Calf, Moses kneeling before the fiery column and Moses giving the Commandments to the people. X. The crossing of the Jordan, the conquest of Jericho, Joshua stopping the course of the sun and Joshua and Eleazar dividing the promised land between the twelve tribes. XI David crowned by Samuel, David's victory over Goliath, David's victory over the Syrians and David sees Bathsheba. XII. Solomon crowned king of Israel by Zadock, the judgement of Solomon, the queen of Sheba before Solomon, and the construction of the Temple. XIII The adoration of the shepherds, the adoration of the Kings, the Baptism of Jesus and the Last Supper.

The execution of these pictures was by Raffael's pupils, Romano, Penni, Giovanni da Udine, Pierino del Vaga.

APPARTAMENTO BORGIA

These rooms were constructed between 1449 and 1455 under Pope Nicholas V. They take their name from the family of the Spanish Pope Alexander VI, whose home they once were. It was he who added the tower. The artistic decoration is by Pinturicchio who between 1492 and 1495 painted five rooms with sybils, apostles, enthroned sciences, legends and stories from the Old and New Testament. The decoration of the Sala dei Pontifici is from the XVIth. cent.

Leo XIII had the rooms restored by Seitz (1889-1897), and they were afterwards thrown open to the public.

Sala delle Sybille. In the twelve lunettes are mural paintings with sybils and prophets. One of the two tapestries represents the Sicilian Vespers, from a sketch by Raffael. It was here that Pope Julian II held Caesar Borgia prisoner. A staircase leads to the Stanzes of Raffael, situated on the next floor.

Sala del Credo. Situated, like the Sala dei Scienze, in the tower. In the twelve lunettes the apostles with scripts on which are written the words of the Credo, painted by Piermatteo d'Amelia, a pupil of Pinturrichio.

Sala delle Scienze e delle Arti Liberali. In the lunettes are allegories of the seven Liberal Arts: Grammar, Dialectic, Geometry, Music, Astrology, Arithmetic and Rhetoric, by Pinturricchio and his pupils. In the arch: Jacob leaving Laban, Lot's flight, Trajan and the widow. There is a remarkable bust of Pope Pious II (1458-1464) by Romano, his contemporary. In this room the buried treasure of Pope Alexander VI was found after his death.

Sala dei Santi. The marvellous murals are by Pinturicchio. The paintings on the ceiling represent the legend of Osiris. Over the door is a Virgin with cherubim. On the back wall the Disputation of St. Catherine. On the wall by the entrance, the martyrdom of St. Barbara and St. Lucy. Opposite on the left St. Paul the Hermit, and St. Antony Abbot. On the right, the Visitation of the Virgin. On the window wall, the martyrdom of St. Sebastian, with the Coliseum and the church of St. Giovanni and Paolo.

Sala dei Pontifici. The superb ceiling with frescos and stuccos is the work of the pupils of Raffael, Giovanni da Udine and Pierino del Vaga. On the walls are tapestries with the story of Cephalos and Procris from the 16th. cent. Pinturicchio painted. In the overhanging curves afftter Raffael's sketches. On the right of an arch is the inscription A (lexander). P (ontifex). M (aximus). VI. The room contains armour and weapons.

THE VATICAN LIBRARY

This world famous library was founded in about 1450 by Pope Nicholas V. It was enlarged by Pope Sixtus IV and transported into the present rooms which were constructed in 1588 by Fontana. The first librarian was Platina, the historian of the Popes.

At the end of the corridor of 340 yards, is the Museo Profano with antique bronzes and a collection of medallions, mosaics and inscriptions. Next comes the Galleria Clementina and the Sala Alessandria with valuable cameos, reliefs and bronze sculptures in the vitrines. The comes the Sala Paolina, the Library of Pope Sixtus V, the Vestibolo della Bibliotheca, the Salone Sixtino, the Sala Sixtina and Galleria di Urbano VIII. The Museo Sacro was founded in 1756 by Pope Benedict XIV to keep the catacomb discoveries. Later the famous Sanctum Sanctorum collection was installed, which is specially rich in enamels and Byzantine treasures. The museum has the following divisions: Sala delle Antiquita Christiane, Sala dei Papyri, The wall-paintings are by von Mengs and Unterberger. Sala degli Indirizzi, Sala delle Adresse di Leo XII e Pia X.

On the right is the room with the «Wedding of the Aldobrandini». Here, too, the famous series of wall-paintings from the Ist. cent. of «The Landscapes of Odysseus», and the «Heroines from the Marancia Gate with the heroines of famous Greek tragedies: Phaedra, Myrrha, Pasiphae, Kanake, there are other wall-paintings from the 3rd. cent. A. D. The Capela di S. Pio V is followed by rooms of Byzantine art and the treasures of the «Sancta Sanctorum».

The great room, called the Salone Sixtino, was constructed by Fontana 1587-1589 under Pope Sixtus V. The walls and arches of the double-naved Aula are decorated with wall-paintings and arabesques of the 17th. cent. In the semi-circles over the windows and at the ends of the arches are views of famous Roman buildings which Pope Sixtus V rennovated or improved. The other paintings celebrate the victorious passage of the book throughout the centuries and the good government of the Pope.

On the walls and the seven columns valuable old manuscripts, designs and coins are to be seen in the beautiful vitrines. Precious gifts from princes and statesmen to the Popes heighten the magnificence of this marvellous hall which is 75 yards long, 17 wide and 10 high.

MICHAELANGELO 1475-1564

The «Giant» came from a very poor Florentine family. He studied painting with Ghirlandajo and sculpture with a pupil of Donatello. For eleven years he studied anatomy. In Florence Lorenzo di Medici became his patron and through him he acquired a good knowledge of the masterpieces of antiquity in good copies.

In 1505 he was summoned to Rome. Julian II charged him with the construction of his tomb. When this project was abandoned to be continued, much later and on a far more modest scale, he received the commission of painting the ceiling of the Sistine Chapel which was inaugurated, after four years of work, on the 31st. Oct. 1512.

In 1514 Leo V was crowned Pope. He favoured his compatriot Michaelangelo and allowed him every demand. He was succeeded by two artistic Popes Hadrian VI and Clement VII. In 1534 Alexander Farnese was at last made Pope Paul III. He declared that he had been waiting thirty years to have Michaelangelo at his disposal. He freed him from the thankless task of Julian II's tomb, and in 1535 appointed him his chief architect, sculptor and painter. He alone knew how to find the way to the heart of this lonely giant. He was also the one whom Michaelangelo genuinely mourned. Then the chisel was once more laid aside and he conjured up the world of spirits and the terror or things to come in his «Last Judgement». After that he painted the Chapel of St. Paul.

In spite of his masterpieces of painting which are unequalled in all Italian art, in spite of his incomparable buildings, he wished only to be thought of as a sculptor. He give its true importance to the the Place of the Capitol (which was designed by him), when he erected the famous esquestrian statue there. When already seventy years old, he was entrusted with the construction of St. Peter's which he continued in the spirit of Bramante and nearly finished.

The sculptures of antiquity had a great influence on his work. He saw in them what was true to life, normal and natural as well as the perfection of art. These works belonged to a world which had disappeared, and he hoped to find a new way. He courageously broke with tradition and started afresh, seeking to heighten Nature into a new life, so that Goethe with fine perception said. that once having seen the works of Michaelangelo, Nature no longer pleased him as he could no longer look upon her with such wonderment.

Michaelangelo was a lonely man. He formed no school around him but he made a school with his works. Strange though it may seem, it was rather his diabolical Power which impelled artist like. Raffael, Sebastiano del Phombo, Tintoretto, Rubens, Caravaggio etc. to follow in his steps.

THE PAINTINGS ON THE CEILING
OF THE SISTINE CHAPEL

In 1481 Pope Sixtus IV summoned the painters Botticelli, Ghirlandajo, Roselli, Perugino, Pinturicchio, Signorelli and others, to paint the Sistine Chapel. From the walls rose twelve frescos representing the Life of Our Lord, and the Story of Moses. Michaelangelo was to paint the Creation and all the previous work, painted with enormous cost by the best painters, had to be removed for this giant work.

It was forced upon him. At first the master refused the honourable task. Three years before, when he was at the height of his sculpturing powers, the Pope had entrusted him with the decoration of his tomb. The mightiest dreams of the sculpture came very near to realisation. For months he had been looking round the stoneyards of Carrara for suitable blocks of marble and suddenly the work was interrupted. A world caved in for him, and Michaelangelo took himself off and refused to return unless his work were restored to him. His friend, Sangallo, brought him back and much against his will he started the new task. Them, a change took place within his artistic mind. Out of the refusal developed a kind of creative intoxication. The vivid flow of figures which were denied to him on the tomb, were now transformed to another medium and ascended the ceiling. This is why one has the impression that the paintings of the Sistine Chapel are, as it were, marbles in terms of paint.

Michaelangelo stresses the drama of the world and its terrible end on the Day of Judgement. He demonstrates the superior forces of Goodness and Light, and even if the fight continues, in the eyes of the Divine Spirit, it is already decided beforehand. The first painting on the ceiling is the beginning and end of all things, that is, God. Michaelangelo has presented the figure of the Creator in more convincing form that has ever been seen before or since. With his creative arms, God is seen groping in Chaos, hurling the planets on their courses, stilling the raging Elements and creating the various forms of life. In the second picture all is changed. A flying figure, he is seen building up the structure of the world. He rises out of the tempest, stetching forth his mighty arms and where his fingers point, the sun and moon begin to shine. In the third picture, the Creator is sailing over the broad expanse of Ocean. He assigns the elements to their proper boundaries and summons the creatures of air and water into life.

Adam and Eve also awaken into life at a look from the Almighty, who gazes earnestly and thoughtfully upon them. How lovely Eve is in the moment of temptation and how hideous afterwards in the Expulsion, following abjecty behind the man who obediently and humbly goes away. She, however, cannot deny herself a last look at the angel. After the Deluge, comes the Thanksgiving of the saved and the sacrifice of Noah. Michaelangelo began his work with the last scene, the Drunkeness of Noah. The magnificent style he developed and the experience he gained was all incorporated into the succeeding work. In the four corners are respectively: The Bronze Snake, The Punishment of Haman, Judith, David and Goliath.

From an artistic point of view the Prophets and Sibyls are Michaelangelos greatest work. Each is a potent force with personality and character. A breath of the Eternal has lain on these figures and, having passed away, they hear inner voices, see great and terrible visions. Deep in mighty thoughts, they seem to feel some indescribable anguish beyond time and place and beyond all human measure. Jonas, upon the altar, has just been vomited forth by the whale. He gazes upon the Lord. Daniel is a jealous impetuous youth. Ezekiel is exalted. He sees God face to face. Isiah has a «Double Face». Joël is thinking of the pain of human suffering. Zacharias is preoccupied with the new Temple, as Pope Julian II was with St. Peter's.

In the Sybils the master did not bother about iconographical details. The old ones are made to appear young and the young Cumaeanis here an age-old woman. He has ommitted the Sybil of the Tibur altogether. They are are placed as complements to the prophets. As with these latter, the sybils have boys assigned to them to bring books and rolls, to light the lamps or offer their backs as lecterns. The Lybian Sybil is a true masterpiece, sitting in a half turned position and just rising from her seat in a way which only Michaelangelo could portray. The Persian Sybil is an old witch, thin, bent and hideous, and yet not unpleasing. The indestructible Cumaean is a thousand years old while the Erythraean, Apollo's sister, is a noble Greek figure.

In the intermediate spaces are the antecedents of Christ. In these the Master has immortalised the ordinary people, the poor, the people from whom Christ himself came and who were beloved by him. The order of the groups is indicated by inscriptions on the windows. In the window picture are represented families consisting of a man, a woman and a child sitting on the ground. The 104 decorative figures, the 46 pairs of figures and the 12 people in the intervening spaces are really pictures of value in themselves and quite equal to the principal figures of the whole. The twenty slaves are among the most beautiful human figures the master ever painted.

The name of Pope Julian II is forever linked with that of the Sistine Chapel. With kindness and indomitable energy he continuously drove the master on, ever fearing that he would not live to see the completed work. He died only a few months after it was finished.

Goethe, on his first trip to Rome visited the Chapel on various occasions. «I had to gaze and marvel. The inner strength and manliness of the master exceeds all expression. Without seeing the Sistine Chapel no one could ever imagine what a single man is capable of».

THE LAST JUDGEMENT

Some time after the painting of the ceiling, from 1534-1541, Michaelangelo painted the Last Judgement, a fresco of about 200 yards. He painted this entirely alone.

The gigantic and furious Judge of the World dominates the picture. His gesture has a commanding power which all and everything must follow. The Blessed Virgin cringes beside him, powerless, and turns away her head. All intervention is in vain. The onlooker seems to be drawn into the events. Are not these our arms raised in supplication? Is not that our body which crouches, seeking to avoid the Judge, groping in the darkness? Is it not our own fear of punishment that makes us tremble and cry out, as we have never cried before? We seem to be hurled through lofty rooms and down into fathomless depths. It is a power which makes us reel, draws us up or throws us down according to the will of the raised and threatening hand. And then we feel a sort of joy that the apparent injustice which seems to govern the world is at any rate over now. That injustice which makes the evil to triumph and the the good to suffer greatly, finds its compensation in that we see a Divine Justice at work here which makes up for all the senseless things we have to live through.

It is impossible to grasp the whole picture in one glance. One has to go over it carefully. On closer inspection, out of what at first seens a confused mass of figures, one can pick out five groups:

1. On the top, angels with instruments of martyrdom.

2. Christ and Mary.

3. On both sides, the chosen, apostles, martyrs, virgins, and confessors.

4. In the lower part (the figures are only half the size of the upper part) the angels of judgement with trumpets to announce the judgement, proceeding earthwards with the books of good works and sins.

5. The resurrection from the dead, with skeletons and all forms of humanity. The blessed mount heavenwards. On the right sinners plead for admittance to heaven but they are repelled by the angels and taken down by the devils. At the Bottom Charon draws the crowd together helped by Minos who is surrounded by snakes. This is a portrait of Biagio da Cesena, the Pope's master of ceremonies. He had declared that the picture was more suited to a tavern than the Pope's chapel on account of the many nude figures. Consequently Michaelangelo punished him with this portrait. He demanded that it should be taken out but Paul III said: «I could perhaps ask for you to be absolved from Purgatory but in Hell there is no Absolution».

Paul IV and Clement VII had some of the figures painted over with clothes. The picture has become rather blackened by incense and candles.

THE BASILICA OF S. GIOVANNI IN LATERANO

The Lateran was the property of the family Laterani until the time of Nero. Nero had the owner killed and took possession of it. Constantine the Great presented it to the bishop of Rome and in this way the Lateran became the residence of the Popes. With the Lateran as «The Cathedral of Bishops of Rome and the mother and head of all the churches of this city and the whole world», the sacred Temple of Jerusalem passed out of power.

Its name has been changed at various times. First it was called the Basilica Constantiniana, later San Salvatore. Gregory the Great called it The Golden Basilica because of its richness, and later on it got the name of its original owner. In 896 the church collapsed and after its restoration it was called after the near-by monastery St. Giovanni in Laterano. In 1308 and 1361 a fire destroyed it again. After his return from French imprisonment Gregory XI had it restored once more. Since then nearly every Pope has devoted himself to its embellishment. Pope Innocent X, in 1650, started alterations with baroque decorations which, unfortunately, changed the aspect of the old church. The colossal statues of the apostles were put in the niches in the time of Pope Clement XI. Clement XII, in 1734, built a new façade and the marvellous Corsini chapel which is a masterpiece full of harmony and splendour. It has a richly ornamented, rounded arch and a cupola over the square tambour. The walls and floors are covered with different coloured marbles. All that remains of the old Basilica are the mosaics of the choir dating from the 13th. cent., and the Leonine Corridor and porticus of the 10th. cent.

The vestibole is 10 yards deep and 55 yards wide. 24 marble columns support a rounded arch decorated with stuccos. An antique statue of Constantine of very little value is placed in here. Five doorways open on to the church. On the extreme right is the Porta Santa. The interior surprises one by its magnificence and the size of the central nave. The marvellous ceiling is said to have been planned by Michalangelo. The floor is a mosaic work of the 15th. cent. In the intersecting nave on the centre of the high altar is the ciborium, a beautiful Gothic work of 1367. It contains the most important relics of the church, the heads of S. Peter and Paul. Beneath is the Altare Papale, on which only the Pope has the right to say mass. It contains a wooden tablet which is said to have been the altar of St. Peter in the catacombs. The Palace and church are extra-territorial and belong to the Vatican. Ever since 1123 councils and synods have been held in this church.

RAFFAEL'S CHRIST. — From the «Disputa del Sacramento» in the Stanza della Segnatura. The great teachers and followers of the church have assembled round the altar with the Sacrament. — Jerome, Pope Gregory the Great, Ambrose, Augustine, Peter Lombardus. Behind them a crowd, worshipping. Over the altar is the Dove of the Holy Ghost and, higher still, enthroned on clouds, is Christ between his Mother and St. John the Baptist. On the cloud on the left are St. Peter, Adam, and St. John the Evangelist, David, St. Stephan, Jeremiah, St. Paul, Abraham, Jacob, Moses and St. Lawrence. The whole conception of the Church has been expressed in a most powerful manner inthis painting which is especially remarkable for its colours.

PARNASSUS. — Stanze della Segnatura. Apollo is seated playing a violin instead of the lyre in front of a Castilian fountain at the foot of Parnassus. Round him are the Muses and the most famous poets and poetesses of Antiquity and modern times. Above all is Homer, behind him, Dante talking to Virgil. Sappho appears as a very beautiful, blonde woman. The world is serene and lovely, filled with noble sciences and arts, illuminated by the Divine Spirit and wisely governed by the laws. This is what Raffael wishes to express in this picture. On the ceiling the Poesia, perhaps the most beautiful of all portraits by Raffael. The woodwork between the pictures is very fine.

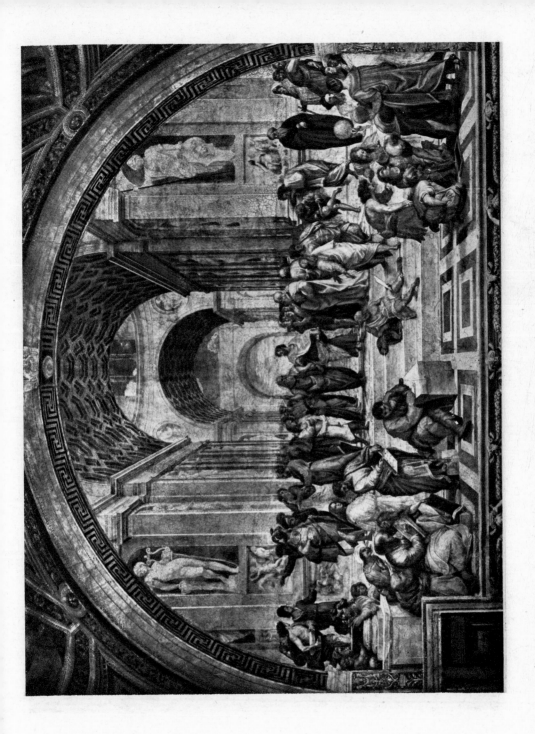

THE SCHOOL OF ATHENS. — Stanze della Segnatura. This picture is the most perfect composition in all painting, and is also a masterpiece of architecture of the high Renaissance. Beneath the arch are Plato and Aristotle debating; on the stairs Diogenes; on the left Socrates teaching and Pythagoras, wrapped in thought; on the right, Archimedes working with a compass and beside him famous men of ancient times and more modern ones. The whole is a triumph of scientific investigation. The seven liberal arts open the way to the highest wisdom, displayed at its best by Aristotle and Plato. Archimedes has the features of Bramante and there is also a self-portrait of Raffael.

THE MASS OF BOLSENA. — Stanza di Eliodoro. A priest who has doubted the miracle of the Transubstantiation is convinced by the apparition of the bleeding host. The contrast between Pope Julian II praying in the certainty of his Dogma, and the priest who bows humbly before the miracle, dominates the whole picture. The miracle flows through the Mass like a spiritual stream. This wall-painting is considered among Raffael's best because of its colours, especially in the harmonious, reddish tones. The miracle of Bolsena took place in 1263, that is some 250 years before Pope Julian II, in the time of Pope Urban IV.

THE LIBERATION OF ST. PETER. — Stanza di Eliodoro. A masterpiece of light and shade. St. Peter is sleeping behind the bars of the prison but his liberation arrives in the shape of an approaching angel whose apparition floods the cell and the sleeping guards with light. The moonlight, the torch, the light round the angel, the relection on the metal of the armour, the clouds and the smoke are all treated with incomparable skill.

THE EXPULSION OF HELIODORUS. — Stanza di Eliodoro. The group of the celestial rider with the youth at his side, arriving to punish the temple thief, Heliodorus is very fine. Heliodorus has sunk to the ground in terror and looks up to the rider whose right hand is raise threateningly. Behind are some of the thief's companions, panic-stricken, while others are still occupied with the loot. Pope Julian II is being carried on the «silla gestoria», an anachronism, as the scene is in the Temple of Jerusalem. The visitors on the lefts, their expressions changing from panic to joyful suprise, are magnificently depicted.

FIRE IN THE BORGO. — Stanza dell'Incendio. Pope Leo XIV, in 847, extinguished a fire near St. Peter's by making the sign of the Cross. This audacious work, chiefly by Raffael, symbolises the power of the Papal blessing. The execution of the work was left to Raffael's pupils. The Loggia with the Pope in the background gives an exact idea of the old Basilica in Raffael's time. On the right is the famous vase carrier.

THE LOGGIAS OF RAFFAEL. — Here the painter become architect as well.
Innumerable figures, plants, beasts and fine stucco surround the paintings and embellish
the columns, the whole being gathered together by the architectural structure. Between
the fruits and flowers round the windows are relief like paintings.

JACOB FINDS RACHEL. — Loggias of Raffael. Jacob left his father's house to find a wife. On the way and near a fountain he met the beautiful Rachel, daughter of his uncle Laban. To win her he enslaved himself for seven years, but on the eve of his wedding, his uncle deceived him by giving him the ugly Lea, his other daughter, and he had to serve seven years more to win Rachel from his wily uncle.

DOOR TO THE LOGGIAS OF POPE GREGORY XIII. — The wise Pope (1572-
1585) came from a noble family of Bologna. He founded 23 colleges at Rome, among
others the Germanicum. The division of time, the Gregorian Calendar, invented by
him is an historical fact of major importance and has given immortality to his name.
The half dragon is his coast-of-arms.

VIEW INTO THE LOGGIAS OF POPE GREGORY XIII.

SALA DELLA MADONNA. — Appartamento Borgia. Also called «Sala dei Misteri della Fede». The mural paintings are scenes from the life of Christ and His Mother by Pinturicchio. Opposite the window are the Annunciation and the Birth of Christ. In the two lunettes on the right are the Adoration of the Magi and the Resurrection of Christ with a marvellously characteristic portrait of Pope Alexander VI. In the lunette on the left are the Assumption of the Virgin and a Cardinal at the tomb of Christ. The lunette over the window represents the Ascension and the Coming of the Holy Ghost. On the ceiling are beautiful decorations, proverbs and medallions.

THE DISPUTATION OF ST. CATHERINE. — Sala dei Santi. Appartamento Borgia. St. Catherine of Alexandria was thrown into gaol by the Emperor Maxentius after declaring, at a sacrifice, that the pagan cult was a fallacy. Fifty learned philosophers who were sent to refute her, came out of the prison converted to christianity. She was tortured on a rack which broke and finally decapitated in 307. Here she is exquisitely portrayed and the oriental prince at her side has also a charm of his own. Behind the emperor's chair is a self-portrait of Pinturicchio with Andrew Palaeologus, emperor of Byzantium. In the background is the arch of triumph of Constantine the Great.

JOHANNES VIII, PALAEOLOGUS. — Sala dei Pontifice. Appartamento Borgia.
He was emperor of Byzantium (1425-1448). The Paeologus were a Byzantine noble
house which came to the throne during the thirteenth century, uniting with the Pope
and Venice against the Turks. Their dominion ended with the successor of Johannes VIII when the Turks captured Constantinople in 1453. The bust is by the Florentine
Filarete, who died in 1469. On the bronze door of St. Peter's, the departure of Johannes VIII from Constantinople is depicted by the same artist.

THE VATICAN LIBRARY (see page 139).

BRONZE HEAD OF NERO. — Vatican Library. At the entrance to the library
is this, the best portrait of the tyrant. The eye and mouth are grim. The unkempt hair
and beard underline the immorality of the emperor (54-68). His first five years were
beneficent, but then his true character appeared. He had his mother and wife put to
death and thereafter everyone who got in his way. He put the blame of the fire of 64
on the Christians and thousands of them were put to death with terrible tortures. Nero
believed himself to be a great artist. He was eventually killed by a liberated slave.

BRONZE HEAD OF AUGUSTUS. — Vatican Library. This masterpiece of Roman portrait art is opposite the bust of Nero. Caesar adopted the young Augustus, and after the assassination of the former, he knew how to further himself by his astuteness. After the defeat of Cleopatra's forces, his opponent, Antony, committed suicide and Augustus was crowned emperor for life by the Senate. He governed 44 years with great success, carrying on wars on the various frontiers with strategy and generally furthering the public funds. He beautified Rome with temples and other public buildings. During his last years he adopted Tiberius, who therefore became his successor.

THE ALDOBRANDINIAN WEDDING. — Vatican Library. Roman wall painting in the style of the ancient Greek paintings of the 4th. cent. A bride is sitting, heavily veiled, in her chamber, waiting for the procession. Aphrodite is beside her consoling her. Charis is preparing a vase with sweet-smelling essences. On the threshold is Hymenaeus, the god of marriage. One girl is trying the cythara while another is occupied with the incense. A third, beautifully clothed, is waiting to conduct the bride. In the interior of the house are her mother and a slave. Goethe had a copy made for his house in Weimar.

THE SALA REGIA. — This room was completed in 1573 by Antonio da Sangallo. As vestibulum of the Sistine Chapel, it was originally intended for audiences of foreign ambassadors and was to give an impression of power in its richness and luxury. More important than the wall paintings by Vasari, Zucchero and others, are the stucco decorations of the arched ceiling. which were begun by Raffael's pupil, Perino del Vaga and finished by Michaelangelo's pupil, Daniel de Volterra. The hall is more than 38 yards long, 13 yards wide and has seven high doors. On the walls and floor are precious marbles.

GALLERIA GEOGRAFICA. — This magnificent hall is 130 yards long and has its name from the numerous topograghical plans of Italian towns painted by Ant. Danti (1580-1583) There are a number of interesting antique busts. The decorations on the ceiling are by a group of artists who worked under the direction of G. Muziano, (1528-1590).

SELF-PORTRAIT BY MICHAELANGELO. — From the «Last Judgement» in
the Sistine Chapel Ht. Bartholomew exhibits the knife with which he was flayed and in
his left hand he holds his skin. It is on this very skin that Michaelangelo has put his
own, satiric portrait. He has a lot of trouble painting this picture as he had taleen on
a task with innumerable difficulties. He was obliged to paint the whole thing bit by
bit from top to bottom on the fresh plaster and only the very slightest corrections were
possible. He refused all help and had to do the work without sketches. Almost
everything had to be improvised on the wall itself and it proved no easy task. The
hundreds of figures, great and small are all worked out to the last detail and this is,
indeed a gigantic work.

THE SISTINE CHAPEL. — This private, papal chapel was constructed 1473-1481 by Giovanni da Dolci, for Pope Sixtus IV. It is a simple room of 45 by 15 yards, with six windows on each side. The painted, architectural structure enhances the basic structure in a most ingenious way. The famous Sistine choir is a noble work as also the marble partition with its fine reliefs from the workshop of Mino da Fiesole of the 15th. cent. On the walls right and left are murals with scenes from the life of Moses and Christ. The marble floor is a remarkable example of 15 th. cent. Roman marble work.

THE CREATION OF MAN. — By Michaelangelo from the Sistine Chapel. God the Father sails over the world which, as he almost touches it, reflects his image and this is the first man. This man extends his arm towards his creator. The angels remain well protected within the shade of God's cloak. Before them rises the greatest marvel, the image of their Lord and Master, the crowning glory of the Creation. They put their heads together and gaze with child-eyed wonder; one looks aside in awe. Most captivating of all is the half figure of a girl upon whose shoulder the Creator rests his arm.

THE DELUGE. — The surface is covered with four scenes. A host of beings crowd and scatter in all directions as the water surges over them. The climax is reached when the water extends to the highest points. In the centre is Noah's Ark at which the refugees are arriving. One boat seems to be sinking and a woman defends it against assailants. Over all hovers the white dove of peace which is the most moving scene of all.

HIEREMIAS

JERMIAH. — Michaelangelo has given this prophet the most gigantic form. It reminds one of the gnarled branches of an age-old oak. This picture expresss all the anguish which he sang in his psalms. Petrified by grief he he sits with his chim sunk into his hand. The features are apathetic, the eyes appear to see nothing and he is a true picture of mourning. The artist has assigned the weeping and lamentation and outwards shows of grief to the prophet's two companions. This Jeremiah — cum — Michaelangelo is a veritable, tragic image of history and one of the profoundest in all art.

THE CUMAEAN SIBYL. — An old Herculean woman with strong arms which are visible through her armless tunic. Her gigantic body symbolizes the millenarian sibyl. Two children are holding up heavy manuscript. She frowns as she reads, straining her short-sighted eyes while her moving lips articulate the words. She is about to pronounce a difficult oracle.

JONAS. — Exhalted by his personality and his destiny, Jonas occupies the space over the main altar. He has just been thrown up by the whale and he raises his head up towards Heaven. Is he giving thanks to God or protesting against his fate on the fish. Much has been written about his ordinary face and expression. His companions arrive, mounted, astonished at the miracle and distressed by the prophet's hard experiences. This is marvellously reveled by the expressions on their faces.

THE DELPHIC SYBIL. — The flowing mantle sweeps from head to foot in a wonderful curving line. The countenance, seen full-face, is filled with the estasy of the divine word, while the figure expresses a strong spiritual energy. The divine inspiration has come upon her during her profound perusals of the scrolls. There is something sad about the mouth and the wide open eyes.

ZACHARIAS. — The only bold prophet. His short-sighted gaze is fixed upon the book which he strains to read. He signifies Pope Julian II who, in 1506 laid the foundation stone of St. Peter's, for Zacharias had charge of the beginning of the Temple in Jerusalem.

EZEKIEL. — This prophet is remarkable oriental in aspect. The artist represents
him looking up from his reading to hear the revelation of his task. He makes a sudden
gesture of surprise and turns in the direction of the angel's finger.

JOEL. — A spiritual face of enormous gravity pondering over human suffering. This is said to be a portait of Bramante, Michaelangelo's worst enemy, and recalls that of Archimedes in Raffael's «School of Athens».

THE PERSIAN SIBYL. — An old and terribly ugly woman searching for the key to the future of humanity in her book Being shortsighted, she reads aloud better to capture the sense of what she reads. She is the very personification of dejection.

ISIAH. — His finger holds open the book of his inspiration. His eyes are still filled with the sleep from which the children seem to have aroused him in order to receive his message. This half turned figure has had a great influence in the world of art. Raffael repeated it in his «Parnassus». It became the prototype of a new movement given to the human body by a very outstanding artist.

THE LAST JUDGEMENT (see page 142-143).

SAN GIOVANNI IN LATERANO. — The mighty façade made entirely out of limestone was built in 1736 by Al Galilei. Over the entrance hall there is a loggia as an upper storey of the same dimensions. The central of the five arches is assigned to the Pope and it is from here that the Pope blesses the people on Ascension Day. The friese rests upon a high balustrade and contains fifteen colossal statues representing Christ, the Saints and the Apostles.

THE INTERIOR OF ST. GIOVANNI IN LATERANO. — The interior with its
five naves, 400 feet long is solemn and dignified. In the niches are apostles from the
school of Bernini. The marvellous ceiling is the work of Giacomo della Porta in the
High Renaissance. The famous 13th. cent. mosaics in the apse were restored under
Pope Leo XIII in 1883. together with the miraculous bust of Christ. The floor is a super
13th. cent. work of the Cosmates.

COURTYARD OF ST. GIOVANNIS IN LATERANO. — The arcades formed by twisted, mosaic columns surmounted by capitals, give access to the sombre quiet of the courtyard. This is a masterpiece of Romanic architecture, built 1220-1230 by the brothers Vasellati. On the walls are antique inscriptions, sarcophagi and reliefs from the old Basilica. The high friese over the columns is decorated with mosaics.

MARYSAS. — Museo Laterano. Athena invented the flute, but having seen her
reflection with inflated cheeks, she destroyed it. Marysas wanted to get it but he stopped
dead before the goddess' spear, without raising his eyes from the ground. This figure,
together with the threatening Athena, was once placed on the Acropolis. It was a work
of Myron who succeeded in one of those most difficult artistic problems here that of presen-
ting arrested movement. The hands are falsely joined.

SOPHOCLES. — Museo Laterano. Sophocles first won the prize at the Poets contest, in 406 B.C. and thereafter remained the leading tragedian of Greece long after his him as we have known him from tradition, beautiful, noble, well-do and accustomed to death even. The Athenians made a statue to him of which this is a copy. Here we see success. Endowed with a cheerful disposition, modest and loveable, he was one of the happiest of beings, beloved of gods and men alike. He belonged to the 5th. cent. B.C.

MEDEA WITH THE DAUGHTERS OF PELIAS. — Museo Laterano. In vengeance for the fact that Pelias would not give up his father's empire to Jason, her lover, the sorceress, Medea, told his daughters that if they cut him into pieces she would make him younger. Thus we see the preparation for this horrible deed. One of the girls places a heavy tripod and beside her, one of her sisters with a sword looks very doubtful about the affair. On the left is Medea dressed as a barbarian. She got her revenge because the daughters murdered their father. Greek relief from the 5th. cent. B. C.

SALA DEI BUSTI

272. Julius Caesar. Lived 100-44 B. C.
274. Augustus. The crown of wheat is an emblem of a brotherhood of priests to which the emperor belonged also.
275. Diadoche. Hellenistic original of 3rd. cent. B. C.
277. Nero as Apollo. Gov. 57-68 A. D.
280. Emperor Titus. Gov. 79-81 A. D.
282. Trajan. Vov. 98-117 A. D.
283. Emperor Hadrianus. Gov. 117-138.
284. Emperor Antonius Pius. Gov. 138-161 A. D.
285. Emperor Marcus Aurelius. Gov. 161-180 A. D.
286. Emperor Lucius Verus. Gov. 161-169.
287. Commodus. 176-192 A. D.
291. Emperor Septimus Severus. Gov. 193-211 A. D.
338. Diadoche, successor to Alexander the Great. Idealised portrait in the style of the 4th. cent. B. C.
341. Globe of the heavens with the signs of the Zodiac. Ist. cent. A. D.
352. Clothed feminine statue imploring protection. Also callad Livia, wife of Augustus. The statue is of a very dramatic spirit. Work of the Ist. cent. A. D.
389. Column made out of three dancing goddesses of the hours. In the style of the 4th. cent. B. C.

BELVEDERE. CORTILE OTTAGONO

Pavilion of Laocoon.

81. Wall of entrance. Relief from the Ara Pacis Augustae. Part of a friese with the inauguration of the altar in 9 B. C.
In a niche: Niobide. Wonderful remains of a group.
Near the entrance: Altar of Augustus. At one side Victoria with a shield, on the other a sacrifice to the Lares. Further on the Glorification of Caesar and a miracle of St. Laurence. From the time of Augustus.

Pavilion of Apollo.

Upon two columns two originals from the Parthenon, 5th. cent. B. C. The bearded head is most probably the mystic king, Erechtheus, from the Acropolis. The other is a head from the Cella friese.

A so-called Idolino, a rare basalt replica of 5th. cent. B. C.

Near the entrance a sarcophagus with the harbour of Ostia on it. 3rd. cent. A. D.

Pavilion of Canova.

Pius VII placed three statue by Canova here in about 1800.

Perseus, an imitation of Apollo, and Creugas and Damoenes. They are technically perfect but cold and without life.

49. On the wall of the entrance; sarcophagus with a battle of amazons. In the centre Achilles is holding the dying Penthesilea. 3rd. cent. A. D.

42. In a niche Venus Felix and Amor. The body of the goddess has been copied after that of Knidos, the head is that of a Roman woman of the 2nd. cent. A. D.

Pavilion of Hermes.

On the left: Head of Athena. A Greek original of the 5th. cent. B. C. in archaic style. Very rare.

Head of Aristogeiton. Copy from 5th. cent. B. C. in archaic style. Aristogeiton wanted to kill the tyrant Hipparch in 514 B. C., in order to restore the republic.

Vestibolo Rotonda.

Altar tomb of T. Ottavio Diadumeno, a famous athlete, by Policlet.

Pavilion of Apoxiomenes.

Altar of the Vicomagistri. Ist. cent. A. D. Represents a procession with beasts, musicians, four porters with statues of the Lares, the spirit of the Emperor, and the four Vicomagistri, the priests of the Larecult. On it are latin inscriptions from the tombs of the Scipios. Beneath, an inscription given to Hercules by L. Mummius after the destruction of Corinth in 146 B. C.

Atrium of the Torso.

Ara Casali. Altar from the 2nd. cent. A. D. The reliefs on the four sides represent: Venus and Mars enchained on the bed. Vulcan, the deceived husband, holding the tongs. The judgement of Paris. The corpse of Hector being dragged round Troy. Tragic scenes about this hero. Mars approaching the sleeping Rhea Sylvia. Rhea Sylvia with the twims. The exposure of the children on the Tiber. The children protected by the wolf. Mars as the father of the Romans.

Sarcophagus of L. C. Scipio Barbato, consul in 98 B. C.

SALA DELLA BIGA

This is a small rotunda with a cupola, constructed in the time of Pius VI, with four niches and eight half columns. It is named after the marble group in the centre. The biga on two wheels, closed in front and open at the back to allow the driver to mount. This is a Roman work of the Ist. cent. A. D. During the Middle Ages it served as a bishop's throne in St. Mark's Church. The lefthand horse was resored in 1788 by A. Franzoni. The decorations, both inside and out, are among the finest Roman decorations that have come down to us.

609, 613, 617. Children's sarcophagus with scenes from the races at the Circus Maximus. The runners are cupids. 3rd. cent. A. D.

621. Sarcophagus with the fateful race between Pelops and Oenomaus. 3rd. cent. A. D.

610. Bacchus with feminine form. Head and body are antique but do not belong together.

611. So-called Alcibiades in fighting position. Also called «The Athleta». Replica of an original attributed to Cresilas. 5th. cent. B. C.

612. Sacrificing Roman. In a richly pleated togo with his head partially veiled, he is pouring a vase of offerings on the altar. One of the finest Roman statues with toga from Ist. cent. A. D.

615. Discobolos. Replica of original by Naukydes, pupil of Policlet. 4th. cent. B. C. It is also attributed to the famous pupil of Phidias, Alkamenes. The beautifully formed boy holds the discus in his left hand, motionless and erect, with his head slightly forward. With his right hand he makes a measuring movement as if awaiting the right moment for his shot.

616. So-called Phokion. A portrait statue clad only in a riding cloak. The head is a replica of a great batlle leader of the 4th. cent. B. C.; the body is that of the Greek statue of Hermes of the 5th. cent. B. C. Replica of the Dioskurides from the time of Augustus. The statue is supposed to be that of Aristomenes.

619. A racing chariot driver wearing a girdle and carrying a curved knife to cut the reins. 2nd. cent. A. D. The head is antique and belongs to another statue.

620. So-called Sextus from Chaerononea. Beautifully draped statue with a strange head.

32, 39. Candelabra from Otricoli. Roman art 2nd. cent. A. C.

Part II.

22. Diana of Ephesus, representing supernatural fertility. Example of the degenerated Roman art of the 3rd. cent. A. D.
28. Sarcophagus of Orestes. Roman after Greek motifs. 2nd. cent. A. D.
44, 51. Candelabra from St. Constance. The base composed of sphinxes, rams and cupids. Roman 3rd. cent. A. D.
72. Sarcophagus with the meeting of Protesilaeus and Laodamia. 2nd. cent. A. D.

Part III. On the walls ten small antique wall-paintings, four nymphs and four satyrs. 2nd. cent. A. D.
12. Mosaic with fruit, fishes and crayfish. 2nd. cent. A. D.
13. Semo Sancos, Italian peasant goddess. Roman replica of archaic original of the 5th. cent. B. C.

Part. IV.

9. Victory leaning against a tree with trophies. Replica of hellenic original of the 3rd. cent. B. C. The head is an antique head of Athena.
30. Sarcophagus with Ariadne found by Bacchus. Roman 2nd. cent. A. D.
93. Boy of the house of Julius Claudius. Perhaps Marcellus, the nephew of Augustus. Roman Ist. cent. A. D.

Part V.

25. Satyr with flute. Replica of an original by Praxiteles.
Statuette of Nemesis from Villa Hadrianus. Replica of an original of 4th. cent. B. C.

Part VI.

Artemis. Replica of an original work by the school of Praxiteles.
5. Statuettes. Perhaps Persephone. Restored as Ceres. Replica of original of 4th. to 3rd. cent. B. C.
8. Sarcophagus. Selene (Diana) secretly visits the sleeping shepherd Endymion whom she loves. Roman 2nd. cent. A. D.
24. Niobide, the youngest of the sons. Replica of an original of 3rd. cent. B. C.
20. Phrygian with bonnet. The composition recalls the school of Praxiteles.
35. Sarcophagus with the stealing of the daughters of the Leucypides by Castor and Pollux. Roman 2nd. cent. A. D.

32. On the back: Fighting Persian. Statuette from Attalus' gift to to the Acropolis after his vicory over the Gauls. The Persian has fallen to his knees but continues to defend himself with his sword. The hellenic original was in bronze. Attalus I was king of Pergamus (Lived 241-197 B. C.).

33. Statuette of Phokion. See Sala delle Biga.

GALLERIA CHIARAMONTI

This museum bears the name of its founder's family, Pope Pius VII, 1800-1823. It consists of the Galleria Chiaramonti itself, the Galleria Lapidaria and the Braccio Nuovo. The Lapidaria contains the collection of inscriptions of the Vatican with over 5,000 pagan and old christian inscriptions. It was started by the Papal archivist Gaetano Marini. The first two galleries are formed by an arm 330 yards long and 7 wide, and were planned by Bramante in order to communicate the Belvedere with the Loggia of Raffael and the Borgia apartments.

Part I. 3. Sarcophagus of C. Junius Euodus. The relief contains the myth of Admetos and Alcestis. She gave herself to Death for her sick husband who was thereafter cured.

Part II. 15. Hephaestus or Vulcan. The god of fire is represented as a Greek craftsman. The bonnet, in the form of an egg, belonged to the guild. Roman replica of Greek original of the school of Phidias.

Part IV. 4. Hygieia and (part of) Asclepius. Replica of originals in the temple of Asclepieion in the island of Kos, from 4th. cent. B. C.

Part V. 3. Armed statue of Antonius Pius. 137-161.

Part XIII. 1. Hermes. Replica of an original of the 5th. cent. B. C.

4. Ganymede with the eagle. Replica of a Greek original from 3rd. cent. B. C.

Part XVII. 3. Silen with a panthercat. Replica as before.

Part XIX. 13, 17. Portrait of a Roman from the late Republic. A marvellously characteristic work of late Roman art.

5. Athena with an owl. Replica of Greek original of 5th. cent. B. C.

Part XXI. 1. Eros bending his bow. Much restored replica of famous bronze by Lysippius of 4th. cent. B. C.

Part XXIII. 16. Relief with Penelope. Her head in her hand. Replica of a Greek original of the 5th. cent. B. C.

Part XXXII. 3. Imprisoned barbarian. Dacien. Roman 2nd. cent. A. D.

Part XXXV. 18. Portrait of a Roman priest sacrificing. Ist. cent. A. D.

Part XXXVI. 3. Statue of an athlete. Roman copy of Greek original of 4th. cent. B. C.

Part XXXVII. Hercules. Replica of Greek original of 4th. cent. B. C.

Part XXXVIII. Remains of famous ships from lake Nemi.

Part XLVII. 7. Portrait of a Roman, thought to be Sulla. Roman-Greek work from 1st. cent. B. D.

Part LVIII. Personification of winter. A feminine figure clad in a cloak with a pine bough in her hand, is lying in the water where fishes and water-birds are caught by cupids. Signifies winter which interrupts fishing and hunting. Roman work in hellenic manner from 2nd. cent. A. D.

Part LIX. 7. Personification of Autumn. Feminine figure. The cupids gathering grapes personify the autumnal occupation of grape-picking. Roman work in hellenic style from 2nd. cent. A. D. found at Acqua Traversa.

Part. XXIX. 4. Emperor Tiberius with sword and sceptre.

THE BRACCIO NUOVO

This room, started under Pope Pius VII by the architect Rafael Stern in 1817 and finished in 1882, is 77 yards long and 9 yards wide. The centre forms an equilateral cross which is closed on the left by a half-arch, and on the right joins on to the Giardino della Pigna. The ceiling is supported by marvellous columns in marble and granite. Right and left are 28 niches for works of art. In the Greek cross there are 15 rectangular niches for statues, overhead 32 high platforms under the roof and below 32 pedestals for busts. The walls are decorated with copies of reliefs from Trajan's arch and that of Marcus Aurelius. On the floor are antique mosaics from excavations at the Marancia Arch. The cupola, ornamented with stuccos, gives light through 12 windows. In front of the entrance is the statue of Pope Pius VII, the founder of the museum.

26. Statue of Titus. The natural head and the togo are very fine. Near the foot is a wave — the symbol of activity. Ist. cent. A. D.
37. Amazon. (See photograph.)
88. Ganymede or Narcissus. Graceful figure from a fountain. On the tree is the name of «Phaedimos», probably the artist. Ist. 2nd. cent. B. C.

Satyr blowing his flute. Replica of Greek original of 4th. cent. B.C.
In the centre of the Hall:

Bust of Julius Caesar. Over it the alabaster urn of the ashes of Livilla, daughter of Germanicus.

On the three columns, three Medusa Masks from the temple of Venus and Roma by Hadrianus. The fourth mask is a stucco reproduction.

41. Bust of Trajan. 98-117.
43. Selene, goddess of the moon. She cautiously approaches Endymion, the shepherd whom she loves. Replica of Greek original from 3rd. cent. B.C.
53. Portrait of a Roman — supposedly Sulla. 1st. cent. A.D.
68. Bust of Ptolomaeus of Numidia. 21-40. A.D.
74. Bust of Hadrian. 117-138.
76. Hera, type of the so-called «Hera Borghese» at Copenhagen. Replica of Greek original of 5th. cent. B.C.
90. Bust of Faustina Minore, wife of Marcus Aurelius. Died 175 A.D.
108. Julia, daughter of Titus.
114. Toga statue with head of Claudius. 41-54 A.D.
118. Bust of Commodus. 176-192.
120. Statue with the head of Lucius Verus. The body is after an original from the 5th. cent. B.C. perhaps by Myron. The Victory and Globe are suplementary.
121. Philippus Arabus. Emperor from 244-249. Of Arabian origin. Marvellous work of the 3rd. cent. A.D.
124. Head of a Dacian from the forum of Trajan.
126. Armed statue of Domitian 81-96. Excellent portrait of this emperor.

MUSEO GREGORIANO ETRUSCO

1st. Room. Sarcophagus, The wall-paintings are copies of those of an Etruscan tomb at Tarquina from the 6th. cent. B.C.
65. Red Sarcophagus. A procession of Roman officials. 3rd. cent. B.C.

2nd. Room. In the vitrines A-K and in the middle of the room finds from the Regolini-Galassi grave, 650-600 B.C. In vitrines L. and M. finds from other graves of 7th. and 6th. cent. B.C.

3rd. Room. Bronzes. Very rich collection of objects in bronze. Candelabra, censers, armour, tripods, mirrors with mythological and other themes engraved on them.
Vitrine C. 105-106. Children's statues with Etruscan texts.
109. Tripod from Vulci. Very elegant Etruscan bronze-work from 6th. cent. B.C.

Vitrine G. 43. Oval Cist from Vulci with representations of fights between Greeks and Amazons. On the handle, a satyr and a nymph riding on two swans. 3rd. cent. B. C.

On the walls reproductions of wall-paintings from a grave in Tarquina.

4th. Room. Terracotta plaques and Etruscan grave urns.
40. Hermes of Tivoli. Red statue from the last republic.

Part II. Vitrine F.

28-32. The famous figures from Tanagra dating back to hellenic times. Sala Guglielmo, one of the most important collections of Etruscan finds from Vulci. Craftsmanship of 7th.-5th. cent. B. C.

5th. Room. Vitrine D.

50. Corinthian vase. Represents the hunting of the Calydonian boars with Atlanta and Meleager. 6th. cent. B. C.

6th. Room. Vitrine K.

30. Achilles and Briseida whom he brought back as booty from the war. 5th. cent. B. C.

On a colum in the centre of the room is a vase with a white edge. It represents the birth of Dionysius, and Hermes giving the young god to a silem and nymphs for his education. Rare and beautiful work of 5th. cent. B. C.

The semi-circle Room. Vitrine M.

7. Vase with Oedipus and the Sphinx. Oedipus anxious to get her secret, and the Sphinx eager to guard it. By Duris, a famous Greek vasepainter of 5th. cent. B. C.

Vitrine M. Vase with Jason being spat at by a dragon. Masterpiece of 5th. cent. B. C.

Vitrine R. 7. In the foreground Triptolemos to whom Demeter is making a gift of flowers and corn for mankind. Zeus looks on in a fatherly way and Hermes awaits the message. 4th. cent. B. C.

Room 8. On the walls copies of wall-paintings from the famous tomb of François at Vulci. Scenes from the Iliad. Outstanding among them the interment of Patrocles on the left. On the right scenes from the battles between the Etruscans and Romans. 3rd. cent. B. C. In the vitrine are works of Italo — Etruscan ceramics of the 4th. — 1st. cent. B. C.

Vitrine V. I. Terracotta with the dying Adonis. Etruscan art 3rd. cent. B. C.

MUSEO GREGORIANO EGIZIO

This museum was founded by Pope Gregory XVI, arranged by the famous Egyptologist P. L. M. Ungarelli and inaugurated in 1839. It contains monuments from the Vatican, from the Museo Capitolino, from the Egyptian sanctuary at the Villa Hadrianus and acquisitions, gifts and finds made by missionaries.

1st. Room. Sarcophagus.

2, 3, 8. Three sarcophagi without covers in black basalt with hieroglyphics. 6th. cent. B. C.

Vitrine A. 5-B, 6. Mummy sarcophagus of the 22nd. dynasty. 10th-8th. cent. B. C.

2nd. Room. Statues.

10-32. Colossal figures of the lionheaded goddess, Sechet, daughter of the sun, with inscriptions of the Pharoah Amenophis III, (1408-1372 B. C.) In black granite.

16. Fragment of an enthroned Ramses II (1292-1225). B. C.) Black Granite.
26. Sitting statue of the Pharoah Seti I (1313-1292 B. C.).
27. Colossal statue of the emperor Ptolomaeus Philadelphus, founder of the Ptolomaean Library at Alexandria, 285-247 B. C.
25. Arsinoe, his wife. Colossal statue in rose granite.
29. Colossal statue of a princess of the Ptolomaean family, about 260 B. C.

3rd. Room.

Greek-Roman replicas nearly all from Hadrian's villa, 2nd. and 3rd. cent. A. D.
119. Personification of the Nile.
121. Marble relief with a procession of the goddess Iris.
56. Plaster cast of the famous Rosetta Stone whose Greek-Egyptian insciptions enabled the hieroglyphic inscriptions to be deciphered.

4th. Room. Of Naophore.
169. Altar fragment of the time of Tutmosis III. (1496-42 B. C.)
195. Kneeling statue of a cavalry general of the Pharoah. Psammetico II. 6th. cent. B. C.

Semi-circular Corridor. 5th. room:

313, 316, 318. Mummy sarcophagus from saitic times. 6th. cent. B. C.
309. Mummy sarcophagus from Roman times, found at Antinoae. There is a Roman woman painted upon the cover.

Vitrine F. 351. Tablet of a guard of the Cheops pyramids. About 2644-2541. The oldest inscription of the museum. In front is a model of Cheops pyramid.

266. Stone slab of Queen Hatshesowe, 1499-1442 B. C. In the foreground the god Amon.

In rooms 6 and 7 small, craftsman like bronzes, jewels, idols, statuettes, amulets and books of death.

In the rooms 8, 9, 10 an important collection of papyri in hieroglyphic and hieratical writing.

MUSEI LATERANENSI

1st. Room:

7. Torso of a nude boy. In the style of Praxitelian Hermes. Replica of Greek original of 4th. cent. B. C.
37. Relief from a fountain. Nymph gives drink to small satyr. In a nearby grotto Pan plays his flute. Romano hellenic of 2nd. cent. A. D.
41. Triumph of an emperor before a temple. The upper part of the relief which is missing here and has been restored in chalk, is in the Museo dei Termi. The restored head of Trajan is an error by Thorwaldsen. Roman of Ist. cent. A. D.
45. Relief. Two boxers. Raffael made a design of it where the missing parts are joined. The design is unfinished. Roman 2nd. cent. A. D.

3rd. Room:

240. Statue of Antinous, represented as the peasant god, Vertumnus.
244. Altar Giustiniani, dedicated to Hercules. Ist. cent. A. D.
245. Relief with the works of Hercules. Ist. cent. A. D.

Room 4.

281. Fragment from a grave-relief. On the upper part a friese with a cockfight. Ist. cent. A. D.
296. Urn from the Via Appia with a design of a cockfight assisted by two children. The winner is on the table and the other dead. 1st. cent. A. D.

5th. Room.

332, 333. Two similar Satyrs each with a young Dionysius on his back. Ist. cent. A. D.
343. Sacrifice to Mithras. Persian myth of the creation. 2nd. cent. A. D.
344. Basalt stag which originally carried an Artemis. Roman copy of Greek original of 4th. cent. B. C.

6th. Room.

The sculptures of this room were discovered in 1840 and 1846 at Cerveteri, and represent members of the Julian and Claudian dynasty of emperors.
350. Colossal statue of Tiberius with the civic crown.
352. Emperor Claudius, 41-54 as Jupiter with the civic crown.
354. Drusus jr. or Germanicus. Ist. cent. B. C.
361. Fragment of a relief with representation of Etruscan gods of the town: Tarquinii, Vulci and Vetulonia in the guise of a bearded man in a tunic, a female figure on a couch and a bearded man with an oar in his left hand. Probably from a monument dedicated to Claudius. Ist. cent. A. D.
345. A and 255. Two sleeping silens. Roman copy of Greek original.

7th. Room. Here are the masterpieces of the museum.

371. Poet of comedies (Menander?) and Muse. Ist. cent. A. D.
375. Resting satyr. Copy from Praxiteles.

389. Triangular base for a tripod with reliefs of dancers and satyrs. New attic relief after an old original from 4th. cent. B. C.

8th. Room. Finds from the Haterier grave near Rome.

9th. Room. On the floor are mosaics from a house discovered on the Aventino.

It represents the floor of a dining room with the remains of a dinner. Designed by «Heraklit» after a very famous work by Sosos of Pergamon, 5th. cent. B. C.

10th. Room.

506. Archaic, female head. Copy of Greek original of 5th. cent. B. C.
569. Remains from a round monument of a tomb. 2nd. cent. A. D.
585. Young, bearded Roman. 3rd. cent. A. D.
643. Bearded man with a Greek helmet. 2nd. cent. A. D.

11th. Room.

674. Polibreasted, Ephesian Diana. 2nd. cent. A. D.
675. Sarcophagus with Adonis. Left, the goodbye; right the wounding and in the centre the death of Adonis. 3rd. cent. A. D.
699. Sarcophagus with the triumph of Dionysius. 3rd. cent. A. D.

12th. Room.

703. Sarcophagus with the Saga of Orestes. 2nd. cent. A. D.
720. Imitation of the Puteal Libonis from the Roman Forum.

13th. Room.

723, 742. Grave reliefs with portraits of a Roman family.
728, 734. Fragments from porphyry statues. Some with togas, others with armour. 3rd. cent. A. D.

15th. Room. Contains monuments from the excavations at Ostia.

Niche with a Silvanus mosaic. Silvanus, god of the woods, with a halo behind his head, bearded and with a knife in his hand. In front of him a dog and on the left an altar. 2nd. cent. A. D.
941. Aphrodite. Bronze statuette. Roman copy of a hellenic original.
942. Vitrine with Roman bronzes.

16th. Room.

952. Wall mosaic with the Rape of the Sabine Women. 2nd. cent. A. D.
956. Wall painting representing a scene from a tragedy: Saturnus eating one of his sons. 2nd. cent. A. D. All the wall-paintings are from a grave at Ostia.
978. Attis, an Asiatic god, lover of Cybele, resting. 2nd. cent. A. D.

ORIGIN OF THE PHOTOGRAPHS

The autor has received:

From the Italian Ministry of Air (1939) Pict. page 17.

From the Italian Ministry for Popular Culture: The pict. on pp. 22, 24, 26, 32, 41, 52, 54, 58, 62, 63, 72, 74, 78, 96, 92, 96, 106, 108, 119, 136, 139, 142, 160, 165, 168, 175, 178, 186.

From the Director General of the Vatican Collections: The pict. on pp. 18, 20, 21, 23, 25, 27, 28, 30, 31, 33 al 40, 48, 64, 71, 84, 111, 114, 115, 118, 132, 135, 151, 152, 167, 171, 181, 187, 188.

From Gabinetto Fotografico Nacionale, Rome: The pict. on pp. 19, 29, 46, 47, 49, 50, 51, 53, 56, 57, 60, 61, 65-70, 73, q6, 77, 79, 82, 83, 85, 87-92, 97, 98, 100-5, 113, 116, 117, 121, 122, 123, 125-29, 131, 134, 146-50, 153, 155-58, 176, 179.

From the Alinari Gallery, Rome: The pict. on pp. 75, 112, 124, 130, 162.

From the Anderson Art Gallery, Rome: The pict. on pp. 19, 45, 59, 81, 99, 140, 141, 143, 163, 169, 174, 183, 184, 185, 189.

CONTENTS